D1308801

# Killing Us Quietly

## Native Americans and HIV/AIDS

IRENE S. VERNON

University of Nebraska Press, Lincoln and London

Parts of chapter 2 appeared as "Facts and Myths of AIDS and Native American Women." Reprinted from the *American Indian Culture and Research Journal*, volume 24, number 3, by permission of the American Indian Studies Center, UCLA. © Regents of the University of California.

Library of Congress Cataloging-in-Publication Data

Vernon, Irene S., 1955–

Killing us quietly : Native Americans and HIV/AIDS / Irene S. Vernon.

p. cm.

Includes bibliographical references and index.

ISBN 0-8032-4668-4 (cloth : alk. paper) — ISBN 0-8032-9624-x (pbk. : alk. paper)

1. Indians of North America — Health risk assessment.

2. Indians of North America — Health and hygiene.   3. Indians of North America — Medical care.

4. AIDS (Disease) — Patients — United States.   5. HIV-positive persons — Medical care — United States.   I. Title.

RA448.5.I5 V47   2001

362.1′969792′0097073 — dc21

2001027440

To all the men, women, and children who are living with HIV/AIDS and to those fighting the spread of the disease

Our struggle is – as it has been for so long – a struggle for survival as a people. We are not being alarmist when we raise the potential of another demographic collapse due to AIDS and the disappearance of entire indigenous cultures. An epidemic which primarily affects those individuals in their most fecund years can destroy a tribe's future. It has happened before in our history and it can happen again. However, we are tough, and we are determined. We will survive the AIDS challenge. We have 30,000 years of experience in America to help us do so.

Ron Rowell, *Executive Director,*
*National Native American AIDS Prevention Center*

# CONTENTS

FIGURES

# PREFACE

Several years ago I was funded by the Tri-Ethnic Center for Prevention Research at Colorado State University to examine a Native American health issue. I had chosen AIDS because I was somewhat familiar with the topic. While doing undergraduate work at the University of California, Berkeley, in the late 1970s and early 1980s, I lived in a house with gay men who became my close friends. I met many of their friends and engaged in many conversations with them. As time passed I noticed that several of my roommates' friends were becoming sick and my friends were attending many funerals. They began to talk about AIDS, a little-understood disease at that time, and the importance of safe sex. I felt great sympathy for my friends, who were trying to understand the disease and its implications for their lives, and have never forgotten their individual acts of compassion and activism.

Despite my initial introduction to HIV/AIDS, I entered the research project for the Tri-Ethnic Center with no idea how it would consume my life or how it would drive me, like many of my Native brothers and sisters, to keep learning more. As I began researching, I became scared about the fate of Native people, particularly our youth. Looking back, I remembered my gay friends and their concerns and activism, as well as my own behaviors and the social and economic factors that placed me also at high risk.

Dr. Paul Farmer's AIDS work and research in Haiti and the United States not only had a powerful effect on me but made me fear the impact of AIDS in Native communities. Years ago Farmer predicated that AIDS in Haiti would not stay within the gay population but would spread rapidly from men to women and from city to countryside. This prediction has come true. Much of what he wrote about Haiti's social and economic conditions could be applied to Native communities, and I feared that the same progression would occur in Indian country. This fear led me to a more active role in HIV/AIDS prevention. Soon I was publishing articles, brochures, and monographs on Native Americans and HIV/AIDS.

My concerns over the fate of Native people eventually led to a long conversation with my good friend Gerald Vizenor (Vizzie), who urged me to write a book. He said, "You know so much, and what you know is so important. You must do it." For a couple of days I struggled over whether I was the person to take on this project. Realizing the importance of the topic and the lack of written sources, I finally agreed. I am glad I did, and I am indebted to Vizzie for his direction, encouragement, and support in this project. Vizzie, this one is for you.

Working on this book has been very time-consuming, and I have many people to thank. First, I must thank the University of Nebraska Press for their strong commitment to this project. I thank the University of Nebraska Advisory Board and their reviewers for their support and assistance. I also thank the editorial staff, particularly Dr. Sarah Disbrow. I'm most grateful to Gary Dunham for his continued enthusiasm and help throughout the publication process. Others that I am indebted to for assistance and financial support include Colorado State University's Center for Applied Studies in American Ethnicity, the English Department, and the Tri-Ethnic Center for Prevention Research. My friends Roe Bubar, Louis Owens, and Luana Ross must also be thanked because when I felt I could not do this book project, they continued to remind me of its social and cultural importance. I am extremely obliged to many friends and colleagues at the Tri-Ethnic Center who have read parts of the manuscript and helped with the interviewing process and charts – Pam Thurman, Barb Plested, Ruth Edwards, Stephen Serrato, and others. I must also thank Jeff Stein (who has been with me through three books) and whose early editorial and research assistance was indispensable.

I was also fortunate to have Dr. Jan Valdez provide editorial assistance and manuscript preparation very early in the book process. Her kind words, critiques, and efficiency were invaluable in moving the book forward. I am extremely grateful to Jan and her hard work. She is clearly deserving of a paragraph of her own. Thanks Jan.

I also want to recognize and express my appreciation to the Native American AIDS organizations and activists whose insights and contributions to this book and to the prevention of the spread of AIDS have been critical. I am truly indebted to them all. Special thanks to the National Native American AIDS Prevention Center, especially Paul Bouey, Bruce Saunkeah, and Ron Rowell; the Native American Women's Resource Center, especially Charon Asetoyer; the American Indian Community House, especially Cissy Elm, who has kept me connected to the concerns on the eastern seaboard; and the Alaska Health Board, especially Joe Cantil, whose sharing of information has touched my heart. I have been honored by their contributions, as well as by the help and direction from other AIDS activists. I feel fortunate to be a small part of a very genuine, wise, compassionate, talented, and resourceful group of women and men who are fighting the spread of HIV/AIDS.

And, to the HIV/AIDS individuals whose contributions and stories have made this book intimate, I am honored and grateful. Your stories have moved me emotionally and your demonstration of strength and endurance in the face of the disease is worth honoring. My heartfelt thanks. And Parousha, without whom I would not have had the opportunity to hear those voices, I thank you.

Ed and Rachel, I have not forgotten you. Please know that I could not have written this book without the patience, love, and support of my family.

KILLING US QUIETLY

# INTRODUCTION

*We are Needed to*
*Keep the Circle Alive*

The devastating impact of introduced diseases on Native Americans is well known. European and African diseases, not warfare, caused the dramatic population drop from approximately five million Native people in 1492 to a low of 250,000 around 1900.[1] Europeans and Africans brought with them "small pox, measles, the bubonic plague, cholera, typhoid, pleurisy, scarlet fever, diphtheria, mumps, whooping cough, colds, pneumonia . . . malaria and yellow fever."[2] Between the sixteenth and the twentieth centuries there were approximately ninety-three serious epidemics among Native people. Epidemics occurred about every four years and caused significant deaths with each passing.[3]

During the first two hundred years after European contact the three greatest killers were smallpox, typhus, and measles.[4] Of these three, small-pox was the most devastating among Native people, who were highly vulnerable to the new virus. In the sixteenth and seventeenth centuries it caused widespread demographic disaster, often killing whole tribes.[5] By the 1800s smallpox mortality rates among tribes ranged from 55 to 90 percent.[6] The impact on Native people reached beyond the death toll to the entire fabric of society, from the loss of leaders and spiritual knowledge to the loss of traditional ways of life.

Today, many refer to AIDS as the new smallpox, due to its potential to eradicate Native populations as effectively as smallpox once did. Because some Native villages, reservations, rancherias, and pueblos are small and isolated, HIV/AIDS could wipe out entire communities if not aggressively addressed. In a recent conversation with an Alaskan alcohol and drug abuse prevention specialist, I was told a story about a young Native Alaskan who impregnated ten young Alaskan women in his village. On its own the story is devastating, but when I thought about the consequences if the young man was HIV/AIDS positive, I shivered, realizing that HIV/AIDS could easily be the next new smallpox. The concern over AIDS in tribal communities was also addressed by the U.S. surgeon general, Dr. David Satchel. He noted how Native Americans have dwindled in numbers historically and that "we, as a community of Americans, cannot afford to lose more lives or cultural riches from American Indian and Alaska Native cultures . . . [and how] HIV/AIDS is a significant threat to these communities."[7]

During past epidemics, however, disease alone was not to blame for high Native mortality rates. Disease became even more lethal when combined with grossly inadequate or total lack of health care. These factors remain a problem today. In 1928 the Meriam Report, a U.S. government–sponsored study, showed that "every activity undertaken by the national government for the promotion of the health of the Indians was below a reasonable standard of efficiency."[8] In response to this report, nursing staffs, health service personnel salaries, and hospital facilities were increased, but health conditions improved only slightly. In the 1930s Native mortality was still 50 percent higher than that of whites.[9]

Success in improving Native health remained limited as a result of economic, social, and political conditions. Slight improvements occurred again after 1955, when the responsibility for Indian health moved from the Bureau of Indian Affairs (with a history of inadequate health care) to the United States Department of Health, Education, and Welfare. This restructuring brought more health services to some Native populations, but problems of access have persisted for many urban and reservation communities.

The Indian Health Service (IHS) continues to be plagued with problems in meeting the needs of tribal people. In 1990 Ronald Rowell, director of the National Native American AIDS Prevention Center (NNAAPC), noted that the IHS continues to lack the appropriate funding to provide effective medical care for both urban and reservation Indians.[10] Charon Asetoyer, director of the Native American Women's Health Center on the Yankton Sioux Reservation, maintains that the IHS on the reservation "has a pretty fair budget for prevention education yet they spend a very small amount of time out in the schools and out in the community . . . over 50 percent of their time is spent in their offices." She believes they need to "contract with community-based organizations and give them the resources necessary to hire outreach workers to get out there and launch the campaign [against HIV/AIDS]."[11] Charles Cambridge, an AIDS researcher and anthropologist, also notes that "efforts by the IHS, which is responsible for Native American health needs, have been ineffective in dealing with alcoholism on the reservations, mainly because of limited resources, and so far, that pattern is being repeated with AIDS."[12]

Recent newspaper articles have stressed that there has been little improvement in the IHS in the last twenty years. Buford Rolin, chair of the National Indian Health Board, told a Senate committee in 1998 that "people are suffering and dying premature deaths, due in large part to reductions in Indian Health Service spending."[13] In addition to lack of funding for IHS, many in the Native health field feel that the IHS does not see AIDS as a priority.

Inefficiency, lack of funding, and neglect of HIV/AIDS issues place thousands of tribal people at great risk. Poor health and lack of access to health care create an ideal situation for the HIV virus to go virtually unchecked. The spread of HIV/AIDS among other ethnic communities has demonstrated how the disease impacts communities with historically poor health and limited access to health care. Statistics support the assumption that HIV/AIDS can spread easily through poor ethnic communities. Since 1992 the increase in the number of people diagnosed with AIDS in the United States each year has been less than 5 percent and is expected to slow further in the coming years (in the mid-1980s AIDS cases increased 65 to 95 percent each year).[14] However, significant increases are still occurring in specific population groups. As indicated in the 1997 Centers for Disease Control and Prevention (CDC) publication HIV/AIDS *Trends,* men and women of color continue to be the most severely affected by AIDS. Although ethnic minorities constitute 25 percent of the total U.S. population, they account for approximately 54 percent of all AIDS cases. AIDS is the leading cause of death for African American women twenty-five to forty-four years of age.[15] While the number of AIDS cases decreased among whites from 60 percent of the yearly reported total in 1985 to 40 percent in 1995, it increased for other races. African Americans accounted for 25 percent of the annual total in 1985 and for 40 percent in 1995. Hispanics accounted for 15 percent of the annual total in 1985 and 19 percent in 1995. The CDC's 1999 year-end report noted that "during the 1990s the epidemic shifted steadily toward a growing proportion of AIDS cases in blacks and Hispanics and in women and toward a decreasing proportion in men who have sex with men."[16] The proportion of cases among Native Americans and Pacific Islanders continues to be less than 1 percent of the total.[17] But a study of drug treatment patients conducted from 1991 to 1994 in New York City, which has the third largest urban Indian population, revealed that the number of Native Americans testing positive was comparable to that of African Americans.[18]

Among Native people, the reportedly low percentage is viewed with great skepticism and concern. Many believe that the epidemic in Indian country is just beginning to show itself. Since many tribal people live in rural reservations and villages, they have been isolated from the infection, which may have protected them from the virus early in the epidemic but may also have prevented an accurate count of AIDS cases among Natives.

Inaccurate reporting of Native people's race/ethnicity to the Centers for Disease Control and Prevention contributes to the skepticism. The National Native American AIDS Prevention Center in Oakland, California, documented challenges faced by health officials in collecting data. These challenges include "racial misclassification, under-reporting, coding errors, inclusion of insufficient population numbers of the racial group to formulate conclusions, regional limitations for this data collection, which cannot be extrapolated to all Indian country, and the omission of Indian data for urban areas, where most reside."[19] Prior to 1988 most states did not even have a category for reporting Native American AIDS cases; they fell under the label "other."[20] The complexities of Indian identity also complicate gathering data because states, tribes, and various agencies have different criteria in determining who is and is not an Indian. Another problem is the lack of reporting by the IHS to state departments of health.[21] In addition, many Native people fail to seek diagnosis due to mistrust of the IHS and the federal and state governments. For others, a long history of hopelessness and the intense personal shame attached to the disease prevent them from getting tested. Recently, on behalf of the federal government, Dr. David Satcher, U.S. surgeon general, acknowledged the concerns of undercounting and under-reporting of Native AIDS cases and noted how the "Indian Health Service and the Centers for Disease Control have been working with community-based organizations to improve prevention and surveillance."[22]

The cumulative number of reported Native American AIDS cases through December 1999 is 2,132.[23] Although the number may seem low, there were only two cases reported in 1984, indicating a disturbing increase. Currently, AIDS is the "eighth leading cause of mortality of Native Americans between 15 and 34 living on or near reservations."[24] Native Americans face the same risk factors as African American women, who, at the turn of the twentieth century, find AIDS to be the leading cause of death. Native people are subject to "roughly the same rate of new AIDS cases as whites. . . . There were about 10 new AIDS cases per 100,000 Indians and Native Alaskans in 1996, compared with 11 new cases per 100,000 whites."[25] Like the movement of AIDS into the Native population, the movement into the general and female population was slow initially but is now astoundingly rapid.

The increase of reported AIDS cases among Native people is not surprising. Natives are considered high risk for contracting HIV not because of their race but because of behaviors such as alcohol and substance abuse in combination with biological, economic, and social factors. Co-factors vary from Native community to Native community, but many exist in all of them.

The most critical risk factor is behavior, as it relates to various forms of substance abuse. For many Native people the main behavioral risks are alcohol abuse and intravenous drug use. The total effect of alcoholism on Natives is staggering. Alcohol-related accident death rates are approximately three times higher among Natives than among the rest of the U.S. population, and deaths from alcohol-related diseases run four times the national average.[26] Chronic disability, unemployment, family disruption, child abuse, and the destruction of tribal unity together demonstrate the devastating impact of alcohol in Indian country.

The relationship between alcohol, Natives, and AIDS cannot be ignored in the fight against the spread of HIV/AIDS. Although alcohol is not a route of transmission for HIV, it plays a critical role in the AIDS epidemic in that, under its influence, protective behaviors are often forgotten or ignored. Alcohol is linked to unprotected sex because it not only decreases inhibitions but alters risk perceptions. Additionally, it places Native people at high risk because of its negative impacts on the body. Alcohol abuse interferes with the body's use of vitamins and minerals, both critical in maintaining a healthy immune system, and it decreases white blood cell counts, inhibiting the body's ability to fight infection.[27]

Another lethal combination is alcohol and drugs – major agents in the spread of HIV/AIDS among minority people, particularly women, whose main exposure category is intravenous drug use or having unprotected sex with an intravenous drug user. The impacts upon the body from intravenous drug use are very similar to those of alcohol abuse. Since 1986 chemical dependency has increased on many reservations, particularly with the introduction of black tar heroin, which "became as cheap as alcohol and almost as available."[28] Like alcohol abuse, drug abuse results in high-risk behaviors that include unprotected sex and the sharing of contaminated needles.

Tribal communities are also at high risk because of the biological conditions found in these communities. Many have high sexually transmitted disease (STD) rates, which indicate high-risk behavior (i.e., unprotected sexual intercourse). In addition, STDs can assist in the transmission of HIV. STDs allow entry for HIV through open sores or microscopic breaks in affected tissue.[29] It is suggested that when a person is infected with an STD, "he/she is two to five times more likely to become infected with HIV."[30] STDs, like AIDS, tend to be diseases of poverty because they are intensified by conditions of economic hardship whereby the poor do not have the money or time to get tested; hence their STDs or HIV infection remains untreated.

Poverty is viewed by many as one of the leading co-factors in the advance of AIDS because conditions of economic hardship create environments of risk. In the United States HIV has moved unobstructed through impoverished communities.[31] Since many Native communities are impoverished, HIV could easily spread rapidly there, too. As indicated in the 1990 census report, 31.6 percent of the Native population lives below the poverty line, compared to an average of 13.1 percent of all other races in the United States, with the median household incomes $19,897 and $30,056 respectively.[32]

Poverty is also a co-factor because it is closely tied to inequality: those who are impoverished are also at the "bottom of society."[33] This social position places Native people at extreme risk because it also limits access to prevention materials, good health care, and proper medical treatment, all of which are essential for the prevention and treatment of AIDS.

Hand in hand with poverty is a host of other factors, such as poor health, poor diet, and related diseases. Native peoples have historically contracted, and continue to contract, almost every disease at higher rates than the general United States population. The overall health condition of Native people is reflected in the fact that approximately one third of the Native population dies before the age of forty-five.[34] Poor health also makes Natives more susceptible to the HIV infection.

Diabetes is one disease related to poor diet that makes Native people vulnerable to HIV infection. Diabetes rates range from 5 percent to 50 percent among tribes and Native communities.[35] It is "a major cause of morbidity and premature mortality" in Native populations.[36] The IHS has noted that diabetic death rates for Native people are 3.3 times the rate for all other races in the United States.[37] Poor diet is not only a factor in diabetes, it can also affect individuals infected with HIV. Poor diet weakens the immune system, which is important in preventing the progression of HIV to AIDS. Diabetes and HIV are related in another alarming way. The Wagner Indian Health Service, which serves the majority of Native Americans on the Yankton Sioux Reservation, has found that some Native diabetics are sharing their needles with drug users.[38] In sum, poverty, diabetes, and the poor diet related to diabetes, are closely tied to the spread of HIV/AIDS as well as to the maintenance of good health.

Another disease commonly linked to poverty and people of color is tuberculosis (TB). An airborne disease, TB occurs frequently in crowded living conditions with poor ventilation. Many Native people live in cramped and sometimes substandard dwellings. Today, TB is twenty-two times more common among Native Americans than among other races in the United States. The IHS noted that from 1992 to 1994 the Native American death rate from tuberculosis was 475 percent greater than that of other races in the United States.[39]

Having both TB and HIV places people in an even more life-threatening situation. If individuals are infected by mycobacterium tuberculosis, they usually remain healthy and develop only a latent infection. However, if they also have HIV they have a greater potential to develop active TB. HIV infection weakens the body and thus assists in the progression from latent to active TB infection. Those with both HIV and TB have a hundred times greater risk of developing active TB than people who are infected with TB alone.

An estimated "fifty percent of persons infected with both HIV and TB are likely to develop active tuberculosis within two years, compared with the lifetime risk of TB of 5–10 percent for persons infected with TB alone."[40] Among people who are infected with HIV in the United States, the rate of TB cases is an alarmingly 40 percent higher than in the general population.[41] In addition, studies demonstrate that the HIV epidemic contributed greatly to the increase in TB cases in the 1980s and 1990s and that mycobacterium tuberculosis "enhances the HIV replication and might accelerate the natural progression of HIV infection."[42] The high rate of TB in Native communities has convinced the National Native American AIDS Prevention Center to test the majority of clients in their case management network for TB prior to enrolling them in case management. The NNAAPC has recognized that "persons infected with HIV are at increased risk for developing TB and [testing them helps] to prevent the transmission and avoidance of multiple-drug resistant mycobacterium tuberculosis organisms."[43] The relationship between HIV and diseases such as diabetes and tuberculosis is increasingly a topic of extreme concern to health officials.

Fighting the spread of HIV/AIDS among Native people requires that service providers pay close attention not only to prevalent diseases but to social conditions such as homophobia. The degree of acceptance, tolerance, or discrimination toward gay/bisexual tribal members varies from location to location, but in many Native communities the treatment of gays/bisexuals reflects the dominant society's negative attitude. Native HIV/AIDS clients have complained that some medical staff are uncomfortable with them, which they feel results in poor-quality health care. Since AIDS is associated with homosexuality, clients often hide their illness to avoid discrimination. This fear and covertness has devastating results: failure to obtain information and treatment and increased infection rates. Hence, Native communities must address the degree of homophobia within their respective communities, particularly since there seems to be a higher rate of bisexuality (which often receives the same prejudice as homosexuality) among Native Americans than among any other ethnic group in the United States.[44]

High rates of trauma, such as sexual molestation and domestic violence, are also present in many Native communities, placing Native people at risk for HIV/AIDS.[45] These traumas are associated with depression, drug abuse, and anxiety disorders; thus it is extremely important for Natives and AIDS organizations to address the levels and extent of individual and community trauma when they address HIV/AIDS issues and concerns.

Another obstacle to HIV/AIDS prevention in Indian country, and a social co-factor that may place them at high risk, is denial. Denial of the dangers and presence of HIV/AIDS continues in urban, rural, and reservation communities. Many still believe that AIDS is a gay white male disease. However, high sexually transmitted disease rates, high substance abuse rates, conditions of poverty, and an increase in AIDS cases clearly refute the idea that Native communities are immune to HIV infection. Several HIV/AIDS infected Natives have noted that tribal communities not only deny that HIV/AIDS is a problem but have also ostracized infected members.[46] These actions create fear and mistrust and, therefore, reluctance to obtain information and services.

Mistrust of government and public health officials is another social cofactor that is an obstacle to prevention. This legacy of mistrust derives from particular tribal histories of deliberate infection and a long history of inferior health care. An experience that made many tribal people mistrust the government was their "gifts" of blankets infected with smallpox.[47] Mistrust also extends to the Indian Health Service (IHS), where confidentiality is an issue, particularly for IHS officials in small tightly knit communities where rumors and innuendo are common. In 1991 a national commission that visited several Native communities and met with AIDS providers, Natives with AIDS, tribal leaders, and community members found that concern about confidentiality was a persistent theme. The commission reported concerns "over the inability of IHS to protect the confidentiality rights of the patient, evidence of breaches of confidentiality, and the lack of anonymous test sites."[48] Although IHS facilities serve a population of 1.5 million Native people, only 9 percent of the American Indian and Alaskan Native AIDS cases were "initially diagnosed at those facilities."[49] Reasons for low numbers may include distrust as well as lack of IHS services in areas with large numbers of Native AIDS cases. Clearly, this history of distrust prohibits many from seeking diagnosis, assistance, and medical attention.

The current situation for Native people is frightening because they face all the leading co-factors that advance the world pandemic of AIDS. Over 30 million people worldwide live with HIV. Most are in the developing world, specifically sub-Saharan Africa and South Asia.[50] Various factors, such as the cost of anteretroviral drugs (approximately ten thousand U.S. dollars per year), poverty, untreated STDs, and poor quality of and limited access to medical treatment contribute to the high numbers of HIV/AIDS in the developing world.[51] It is also believed that "the lack of HIV education, awareness, prevention and testing services inhibits the ability of people in this vulnerable region [sub-Saharan Africa] to protect themselves, each other and the children they someday may have."[52] With the same overarching poverty, discrimination, and high-risk factors, Native people could confront a new epidemic – AIDS – possibly killing entire communities. Some communities are more aware than others of the potential problems. In New York, for example, the Native American Leadership Commission on Health and AIDS acknowledges that AIDS has the ability to alter Native American communities as much as smallpox did in the sixteenth and seventeenth centuries. Members of the commission realize that their ancestors were not prepared, and that they "can not afford to be unprepared for AIDS" because their survival is at stake.[53] It is clear that at the opening of the twenty-first century, we need to move forward by building partnerships in the fight against AIDS locally and abroad.

*Killing Us Quietly* addresses the critical topic of Native Americans and HIV/AIDS with the goal of educating the general audience as well as sharing information with health officials and health care workers. The first three chapters examine specific target groups in turn: men, women, and youth, detailing their unique situations and needs. Each chapter focuses on particular aspects of HIV/AIDS risk behaviors and co-factors, culturally specific concerns, and urban and isolation issues. These topics are applicable, but not exclusive, to the group under discussion. For example, chapter 1 discusses the concept of two-spirits in relation to Native gay/bisexual men, but that does not mean the concept pertains to them only. There are two-spirit men, women, and youth. Also relevant to all three groups is the issue of poverty, which is stressed in chapter 2.

Each chapter also discusses one or several Native AIDS organizations with long-standing experience in providing health care and other services to their target group. Personal interviews with Natives that have HIV/AIDS are also included. The intimate portraits reveal common and diverging experiences. These individuals live in various settings, their paths toward infection are distinct, and they have faced different types of discrimination and concerns. Although I was given permission to use their names in this book, after much consideration I chose not to. I felt that there remains in the United States and in Indian country a strong stigma attached to HIV/AIDS and I did not want ill will to fall upon these individuals or their families. Therefore, I have used aliases for their names. I also did not use the name of their tribe, substituting instead the name of the state where their tribe is located.

The first chapter examines the group with the largest number of AIDS cases – two-spirit or gay/bisexual men. This chapter describes the traditional and contemporary roles of two-spirit men in Native communities and presents the AIDS epidemic from their perspectives. A discussion of Native demographics helps contextualize the rise of AIDS in urban areas, and urban issues are addressed. The National Native American AIDS Prevention Center in Oakland, California, is profiled because it is the only national organization and serves a large Native gay/bisexual population. Introduced at the beginning of the chapter are personal narratives of Native two-spirit men living in California, a state with one of the highest rates of Native American AIDS cases.

Chapter 2 begins with personal narratives from HIV/AIDS-infected women discussing their unique experiences. The chapter then explores traditional and contemporary roles of Native American women and presents the AIDS epidemic from their perspectives. Increasingly, the face of AIDS is a woman's face, and more specifically, a poor woman's. Globally, women represent 40 percent of adults infected with HIV, and women are the fastest growing group of HIV/AIDS-infected individuals in the United States. Since 1989 the number of reported AIDS cases among Native American women has increased more than tenfold. Women's concerns, such as poverty, menopause, and domestic violence, are addressed. This chapter also includes a description of the Native American Women's Center in Lake Andes, South Dakota, the first women's center located on a reservation that specifically addresses Native women and HIV/AIDS.

A study of HIV/AIDS would be incomplete without an understanding of how it impacts the future of tribal people and communities, particularly the children. Beginning with the story of a young man who contracted the HIV infection during his teens, chapter 3 delves into the issues of HIV/AIDS and Native youth. Native American children throughout the United States suffer from poverty, substance abuse, emotional and physical abuse, and neglect in numbers greater than in the general population. All of these factors place them in danger of acquiring HIV. Native youth live in a variety of situations. Some live on reservations and others live in cities and rural areas. Some are homeless and others come from tightly knit families. Since they belong to one or more of the five hundred plus tribes with different beliefs and cultures, they all have different needs. The chapter examines AIDS among Native youth with special attention paid to youth issues such as adolescent development. The issues affecting Alaskan youth are highlighted because their needs are unique to their isolation in extremely rural areas. Alaskan Natives are also a focus because they have high rates of AIDS, high sexually transmitted disease rates, high rates of child abuse, and one of the highest fetal alcohol syndrome rates in the world.

This chapter also describes a variety of Native organizations that work on youth issues: American Indian Community House in New York, the Minnesota Native American AIDS Task Force, and the Alaska Native Health Board AIDS Awareness Project in Anchorage. Interspersed are stories of HIV/AIDS-positive individuals who contracted the disease during their youth.

*Killing Us Quietly* concludes with a chapter on Native prevention strategies. The chapter offers an overview of the various approaches to serving tribal people and communities that face either high risk for HIV or high HIV rates. The purpose is not to evaluate the quality or benefits of these prevention approaches, but to present an overview of the various approaches. A list of resources valuable to the study of HIV/AIDS in Native communities, including Native American AIDS videos and organizations, follow the chapter.

As the first book on Native Americans and AIDS, *Killing Us Quietly* touches only the tip of the iceberg. The complexity and variety of issues related to HIV/AIDS in Native communities – and the impacts on individuals and communities – are too numerous for any one book. As an introduction to AIDS in Native communities, this book will serve, I hope, as an impetus for others to do more research. Important areas of study include Native women, men, and children, HIV/AIDS in prison, obstacles to risk reduction, HIV/AIDS funding, substance abuse, medical care, and clinical trials. Another important research area is the structures within in United States that allow for HIV/AIDS to spread. It is critical that we work together to provide a sound base for understanding the current and potential impacts in tribal communities and among tribal people.

In addition, I hope that *Killing Us Quietly* will create a forum for Native people in the debates about AIDS and serve as a guide to Native self-empowerment and survival. The challenge for Native people is to address this critical problem – testing our tolerance, biases, and faith in the future – and I believe we will rise to the call. For over five hundred years we have overcome near annihilation and survived in this society. I believe tribal people have what it takes to survive – humanity, love, hope, community, and compassion. As we move into the twenty-first century, we must come together to address this threatening health issue. And by doing so, we will not only be addressing the spread of HIV/AIDS but the overall status of tribal people. By working to stop the spread of HIV "the health status of ALL tribal people will be raised," and a better understanding of the meaning of humanity achieved.[54]

We must all do what we can. For example, we must participate in the planning process and be politically involved. By "sitting at the table," argues Joan Benoit, director of the Native American AIDS Project, our voices will not be "overlooked, silenced, or denied."[55] Through independent effort and the combined targeted efforts of individuals, tribes, organizations, states, governments, health officials, and academics, we will not die silently or quietly.

# NATIVE AMERICAN MEN
## AND HIV/AIDS

*A Distinct People*

Gay/bisexual men, or two-spirits, have the highest infection rate among tribal people. The stories of three two-spirits, Tom, Jordan, and Stephen, illustrate many of the problems and concerns common to this group. They were all infected by having sex with men, the most prevalent form of transmission among two-spirits. Although infected similarly they are in different stages of the disease and they have responded differently to their diagnosis. Their stories reveal many of the issues raised in this chapter, including homelessness, identity, and relationships.

TOM

Tom was placed in an orphanage as an infant. He is a Native American mixed-blood from the Plains and Southeast. During his early childhood he was placed with an upper-middle-class white foster family, who provided all his basic needs and more. He was happy in the foster home. His life changed, however, at age eleven when a single foreign-language teacher in Kansas adopted him and another Native American boy. His adoptive father married three years later.

It was too difficult for Tom to make the transition from the foster family to the adoptive family, and he ran away about thirty times from age eleven to fifteen. He desperately wanted to return to Chicago but did not know how to get there. His life was troubled and he began to get into more and more trouble. He fought authority the entire time he was at his Kansas home and was sent to prison when he turned seventeen. He was in prison for thirteen years.

Prison life proved to be more difficult than his life in Kansas. He was raped and contracted hepatitis C. He also learned that many people were attracted to his strong, beautiful Indian features, and he learned to survive in "the joint" by using his body. His experience in prison taught him other things as well. He earned his associate of arts degree, took computer and architect design courses, received food service training, and worked nine years in the electric shop.

When Tom got out of prison he immediately moved to California and began associating with other Natives. The Natives he "hooked up" with, however, were not positive role models and all drank excessively. Since he had no job, he used what he learned in prison to survive – his body. Tom reflected on his prison experience and said, "I used my body to get friends, get money, and get what I needed." He knew when he got to California that he was still pretty. "I had long hair and a nice face so I began to work the streets prostituting myself and made good money, five hundred dollars per day."

While prostituting, he became aware of HIV. Friends and health agencies told him that it was important to get tested because he was turning five to six tricks a day without sexual protection. His attitude was that he really didn't care much about anything and wasn't worried if he got the virus because he was going to "live my life, enjoy it." However, once he was diagnosed with HIV he could not deal with his positive diagnosis and responded by drinking more, smoking crack, and experimenting with other kinds of drugs. He realized that talking about having AIDS was one thing, but "knowing how to deal with it" was another. He returned to some of his "bad ways" and ended up in jail once again for stealing a car.

While in prison his HIV infection was continually monitored, and his T-cell count remained steady. But a month after getting out of the joint his T-cell count dropped, and he responded the only way he knew – he "went on another little binge for a month." Responding positively in the face of the virus was difficult for Tom, in part because he was a loner who found it difficult to make meaningful friends.

Today, Tom is homeless. He sleeps in a jeep with a good friend who is around ten years older and who tries to take care of him. Tom considers sleeping in a jeep "a lot better than sleeping out on the street in a sleeping bag." Although homeless, he "tries not to look homeless" because he does not like people looking at him in a negative and condescending way.

Recently, Tom has been pondering death because several of his Indian friends have died of AIDS. He also wonders about his own death, about who will claim his body at the morgue and who will attend his funeral. He told his friends that "when I die I don't want to just be dead, I want to have people at my funeral."

Tom wants a better life and to know that he matters in the world. He is attempting to locate and obtain proper housing with the help of AIDS agencies. He also wants to be employed but has found it difficult to get a job. He used to be a manager at a Denny's in Kansas but realizes that getting a job in the food service area as an ex-felon with HIV is difficult, if not impossible. He keeps trying and is currently using a state agency that looks for jobs for HIV-positive individuals. He no longer prostitutes because he is on parole and cannot afford to get caught.

Being healthy is another of Tom's concerns. He is currently attempting to treat both his hepatitis C and HIV infections. He tried one set of cocktail drugs but the side effects were too difficult to handle so he went off them. He is getting ready, however, to try them again. Tom has also sworn off drugs but still drinks.

Although disconnected with his biological, foster, and adoptive families, he has found a family on the street, a family that consists of many other tribal people. He has shared his diagnosis with them and feels that they are supportive and "comfortable with it." Feeling a sense of Native identity, Tom also tries to find strength in attending powwows, which bring back memories of when he used to fancy dance as a twelve year old.

Tom is doing the best he can with limited resources, and he praises the Native and non-Native AIDS agencies for the work they do and for helping him see a future. He told me that what he wants in his future is to be employed, to get more education, and to have an apartment. He also wants to leave San Francisco for some place close but less expensive. He does not want to leave the area because he feels that it is one of the best areas for HIV treatment and care. Admirably, Tom also feels an obligation to give back to the community, and he wants to join "some kind of lecture circuit." He would like to talk to juveniles about HIV and teach them how to handle a positive diagnosis.

JORDAN

Jordan was born to parents who were poor but had "enough sense to go out and get a high school diploma." He also comes from a family of strong women. His great-grandmother was a well-respected tribal leader and his mother, who is black and Native American and was born in Nevada, was the youngest of nine siblings and endured the Indian boarding school experience. She suffered lots of discrimination because of her mixed-blood identity. In searching and exploring his own mixed-blood identity, Jordan recently visited his mother's reservation and met with relatives and tribal elders. He continues to keep limited contact with his tribal relatives from Nevada and Oregon.

Diagnosed with HIV infection three months ago, Jordan is just beginning to process the information. He talks about viewing AIDS as another part of life, as "another aspect of us, it's like death." He is trying not to let it define who he is. His HIV diagnosis came as a surprise to Jordan because he considered himself aware, and mostly participated in careful and safe sex. He did not have lots of sexual partners and had yearly tests. Previous to his diagnosis he had a six-year relationship with an HIV-infected man. They had protected sex for one year and then the remaining part of their relationship was without sex. During this time Jordan tested himself regularly with negative results.

He contracted the disease from his most recent partner, whom he loved and had unprotected sex with. Jordan's partner had the infection and did not tell Jordan until he had been with him for a while. Jordan was upset that his partner had not told him sooner and as a result he ended the relationship. Jordan looks back at this relationship as "looking for love in all the wrong places" and knows that he was in it because of his need to be loved. He has wondered if his early childhood experiences and his struggles to "be himself" and be accepted for who he is (gay/bisexual, black, and Native American) made him look for love in all the wrong places.

When speaking of his anger about his diagnosis, Jordan feels angrier with himself than with his partner, whom he sympathizes with. He told me that his ex-partner was an abused child, his mother had died of a heroine overdose when he was twelve, and his father was in prison. Jordan's emotions toward the man who gave him HIV bounce back and forth from anger to love.

In the three months since his diagnosis, Jordan has given a lot of thought to life and the disease he carries, and he attempts to "embrace it." He says, "I want my experiences to be beautiful because I am a beautiful person." He follows the teachings of his mother, whom he highly respects and who taught him to look at the beauty of life. Jordan chooses not to be a victim of his disease. Trained as a long-distance runner, he continues to participate in marathons and takes care of his mind, body, and soul. He thinks and acts positively, believing that positive thinking "empowers people." And he continues to work as a kindergarten teacher.

However, he retains a sense of loneliness in his struggle. With all his positive thinking, Jordan still feels that "there's something that won't allow me to tell people that I am HIV positive because of people's stupidity." He has only told seven people of his diagnosis. His respect, love, and admiration for his mother made her one of the seven. He said he had a "hard time telling" her but she showed him love and support.

Jordan grapples with wanting to tell people and wanting to be with people: "I feel hurt about my HIV and get angry at times when I think that I can't bring somebody [home] with me." He talks about his need to be with someone as a game where he will, at times, not want it but then feel he needs it. So he goes out looking for someone, and then makes himself go home without someone to be intimate with. Jordan thinks about sex, his duty to tell people about his infection, and his wants, needs, and desires. Presently, he is placing his carnal needs second to his spiritual needs by actively making a choice to "put energy into my spirit, as opposed to my flesh and body."

As Jordan faces his changing lifestyle and demise, he has found comfort at the Urban Indian Health Center in San Francisco. He is aware of the stigma attached to the disease, so he prefers to be with people of color who are faced with the same issues as he is. He talked about a sense of common understanding among them.


STEPHEN

Stephen was born in California although he has very close ties to his reservation in Idaho, where he lived for several years. Married once to a woman who did drugs, Stephen has been in a long-term relationship with a man whom he considers his husband. When he was young he considered himself "wild" and engaged in high-risk behaviors. These behaviors have been tempered since diagnosis but have not stopped completely. Stephen notes that his status has "slowed me down big time." He feels that he can not party any more and needs to watch what he does and whom he is with. Yet, he adds, in some ways his life "has gotten better."

Diagnosed with HIV a year ago, Stephen has not told his entire family. He mentioned that he did not want to tell his mother because she has already been through so much and he "was a hard kid growing up." His mother actually asked him if he had HIV and he told her that he didn't. He has told his brother, who has been supportive and has said that his family "already knows" but doesn't talk to him about it.

He believes that he may have contracted the virus either from his wife or from his husband, whom he has been with for six years. His husband was diagnosed with HIV ten years ago and although Stephen was aware of his status, he was inconsistent with protection. When asked why he did not protect himself he responded, "I love him and this is where it is going to stop." He added, "this is going to be my last one [relationship] before I go out." In retrospect he thinks that he would have acted differently if he had more information on HIV/AIDS and also believes that people today should "be careful because it ain't worth it." It is advice he learned the hard way.

As a self-employed business owner Stephen has not made the effort to participate in a variety of HIV/AIDS services. He explains that "running my own business I don't have time for all that." However, he does utilize the Urban Indian Health Center in San Francisco as well as attend powwows and sweats on the reservation. He visits the "rez" frequently and he has noticed that his tribe is aware of HIV and has a strong program for educational outreach. He feels completely supported by his tribe and says that they openly discuss HIV/AIDS. "Anybody that goes onto the rez will find out about AIDS, one way or another," Stephen says, "because all the aunts and uncles and grandfathers get together and they all talk about it." Stephen commented that it is common conversation at the dinner table, and he adds, "it's just their [tribal elders] job – that is what they do, to counsel other Indians about it."

Stephen mentioned that his tribe's response to HIV is not true for all tribes and that "other tribes do not want to talk about it. They keep everything hush hush." He believes that other tribes do not openly discuss this deadly disease because Indian people "just don't care, because the white people have just taken too much from them" and it has left them with a sense of hopelessness. He thinks there are forces that "keep them in one little spot, keep them down" and do not let them be strong.

The stories of Tom, Jordan, and Stephen demonstrate the difficulties HIV-infected men face, and the importance of human emotions such as the need to be loved and feel loved. These men contracted HIV from partners whom they loved or felt loved by, and it is critical that society comes to terms with the importance of satisfying one's need for intimacy to understand the fight against the spread of HIV.

After two decades of confronting the HIV/AIDS epidemic in the United States, the challenge is still upon us but the fight has changed. The number of new cases each year is declining, and combination drug therapy is allowing those with HIV/AIDS to live longer. The declining numbers and advances in treatment, however, are creating a false sense of complacency in some. Thousands still become infected each year, and thousands will continue to die.

The recommendations for safe sexual practices, which early in the epidemic were aimed at "white gay men," are being changed to reflect the complex web of the disease and the way it has moved into the heterosexual, female, and adolescent communities. But these messages are not holding

Fig 1. AIDS cases and Native American AIDS cases, by gender

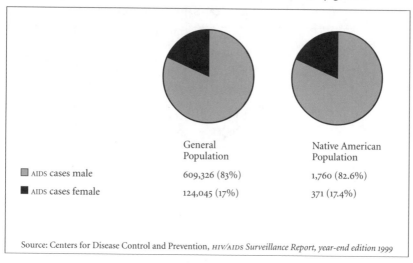

|  | General Population | Native American Population |
|---|---|---|
| ■ AIDS cases male | 609,326 (83%) | 1,760 (82.6%) |
| ■ AIDS cases female | 124,045 (17%) | 371 (17.4%) |

Source: Centers for Disease Control and Prevention, HIV/AIDS Surveillance Report, year-end edition 1999

the attention of the young, who still believe that it is an "older gay man's disease." Also, the new and older gay/bisexual populations are not adhering to safe sexual practices. Particularly alarming is the fact that while numbers are declining for the general population, rates are increasing among minority populations. This tells us we must try to understand the various factors allowing HIV/AIDS to continue to spread among minority populations and to devise appropriate strategies for different populations. We must pay diligent attention to this deadly disease, particularly to the ways in which it is now impacting minority communities. It is time to address the needs of those who have been marginalized in the debate over HIV/AIDS and are witnessing the effects of the failure to address their needs.

This chapter examines the cultural setting and variables that have contributed to the spread of HIV/AIDS among Native American men. It argues that developing strategies for combating HIV/AIDS must consider the cultural context of the disease and the specific barriers to effective health care and prevention that Native men face. I conclude with a discussion of some effective programs that can serve as models for other programs to meet the needs of Native men.

As of December 1999 males accounted for 83 percent of AIDS cases in the United States, with 56 percent of the adult/adolescent population infected through men having sex with men (figs. 1 and 2). The pattern in the

Fig 2. Male adult/adolescent and Native American male adult/adolescent AIDS cases, by exposure category

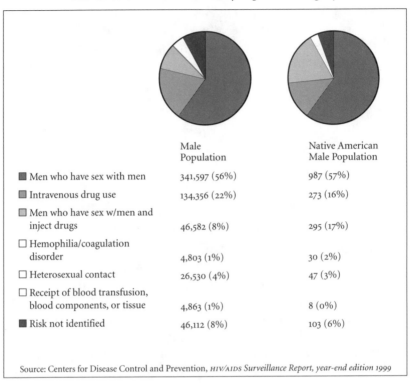

| | Male Population | Native American Male Population |
|---|---|---|
| ■ Men who have sex with men | 341,597 (56%) | 987 (57%) |
| ■ Intravenous drug use | 134,356 (22%) | 273 (16%) |
| ■ Men who have sex w/men and inject drugs | 46,582 (8%) | 295 (17%) |
| ☐ Hemophilia/coagulation disorder | 4,803 (1%) | 30 (2%) |
| ☐ Heterosexual contact | 26,530 (4%) | 47 (3%) |
| ☐ Receipt of blood transfusion, blood components, or tissue | 4,863 (1%) | 8 (0%) |
| ■ Risk not identified | 46,112 (8%) | 103 (6%) |

Source: Centers for Disease Control and Prevention, *HIV/AIDS Surveillance Report, year-end edition 1999*

Native population is similar to that of society at large, with men representing 82.6 percent of the cases and men who have sex with men constituting the largest segment of Native American AIDS cases, 57 percent. The second largest exposure category for Native male adult/adolescents is men who have sex with men and inject drugs, 17 percent. Since males account for the largest portion of AIDS cases for Native Americans, and men who have sex with men make up the main exposure category, it is critical that we focus our attention on this population to stop the further spread of HIV/AIDS in tribal communities.

We must also keep in mind that the rates of heterosexual transmission are increasing, and the growing number of males infected increases the exposure chances for women. Also, the use of intravenous drugs and practices such as sharing needles are other means of spreading HIV/AIDS from infected men to the wider Native population. David, for example, a heterosexual tribal member from the eastern seaboard, contracted the virus through intravenous drug use. Sadly, he shared needles and never practiced safe sex. When he finally took an HIV/AIDS test he already had full-blown AIDS. Upon his diagnosis he went into complete denial, drinking and smoking crack and then engaging in unprotected sex with several prostitutes. David's story is not unusual in either the method of transmission or the response to diagnosis. Therefore, it is also important to examine and understand the complexities of infection among the male population in general.

To address the issue of HIV/AIDS, particularly among two-spirits, it is necessary to understand the complexities of gender roles and sexual diversity in Native societies. Since the goal is to work toward changing high-risk behavior, we must understand that behavior in order to change it.

Knowledge of gender and sexual variance in Native societies is limited, but what is known is that some tribal communities had more than male and female genders and participated in a variety of sexual orientations. Those tribal members who engaged in third and fourth genders and sexual diversification were known by several names, such as *winkte* (Lakota), *nádleeh* (Navajo), *kwidó* (Tewa), *tainna wa'ippe* (Shoshone), *dubuds* (Paiute), *lhamana* (Zuni), *warharmi* (Kamia), *hwame* (Mohave), and *hemaneh* (Algonquian-speaking Cheyenne).[1]

In this work I follow the definitions of gender, sex, and sexualities that can be found in Sue-Ellen Jacob's book, *Two-Spirit People: Native American Gender Identity, Sexuality, and Spirituality.* She applies the term *gender* "specifically to cultural rules, ideologies, and expected behaviors for individuals of diverse phenotypes and psychosocial characteristics"; the term *sex* to "biological phenotypes"; and the term *sexualities* to "the range of behaviors called 'homosexuality,' 'heterosexuality,' 'bisexuality,' 'trisexuality,' and the like."[2] The importance in understanding the complex area of Native gender and sexuality is that, for example, in some tribal traditions a third-gender male-bodied person would not have sex with another third-gender male-bodied person because it would be considered homosexuality. Yet this same person would have sex with a "straight" or male-bodied man, which would be considered heterosexual sex within that Native culture.[3] In American society, however, his act would be classified as homosexual. Understanding these cultural complexities is critical in HIV/AIDS prevention and intervention programs because if materials are designed to address homosexual behavior, some tribal people will ignore it because they would not consider their male-male sexual behavior as homosexual acts.

Historically, the status of men who had sex with men varied in Native societies, but in most tribes these men were accepted because Native world views and philosophies honored and respected all beings – beings were sacred and important to the unity of life.[4] This philosophy changed, however, with colonization. After European contact and the imposition of Christian values and morals on tribal societies, gender behaviors that were accepted as normal aspects of tribal life became viewed as deviant and immoral.[5] Europeans brought with them the belief that sex was solely procreative, and any divergence was seen as an act against nature and God. The Spanish had Natives burned to death and fed to the dogs if they were found to have engaged in same-sex relations or if they even dressed inappropriately.[6] Americans continued the persecution, forcing tribal people by law to conform to the Judeo-Christian determination of acceptable human behavior.[7]

Two commonly used terms today for Native men who have sex with men are *berdache* and *two-spirit*. The word *berdache* originated in Persia (via the Arabs), was adopted into the Italian language, and appeared in Spain and France around the sixteenth century. The French dictionary of 1680 defined *bardaje* as "a young man who is shamefully abused."[8] It has been used by anthropologists to describe homosexual activity among tribal people.[9] The word *berdache* has a long history and a variety of negative meanings, although some anthropologists argue that the word has "lost its derogatory meaning," particularly in America.[10] To many Native people, however, *berdache* contains a negative connotation and does not express the complexity of gender diversity found within Native societies.[11]

The term *two-spirit* is derived from the Algonquian *niizh manitoag* and refers to a human being with both masculine and feminine qualities that are simultaneously manifested in a variety of ways.[12] This term has a meaning beyond sexual orientation, suggesting an acceptance and recognition of such an individual's place and role in the community. The term has come to be used among many tribes to describe contemporary Native gays/lesbians/bisexuals, transvestites, transgenders, and cross-dressers.[13] Members of the Two-Spirit Society of Colorado maintain that *two-spirit* is a contemporary term and a philosophy that is continually being developed, as well as a recognition of their place in the circle of life.[14] I have chosen to use it because it suggests the uniqueness of Native men who have sex with men, and it is commonly accepted as a generic term by the target group with the highest percentage of AIDS infection.[15] I am, however, aware that it is not entirely accepted by all Native gay/bisexual men, particularly those who identify themselves through their own tribal terms, yet it allows me to categorize the distinctiveness of their being that is different from what is commonly accepted about gay/bisexual men.

There remain remnants of respect for Natives with alternative genders and sexual orientation, particularly among traditionalists who remember the place of alternative genders and behaviors in their communities.[16] Today, however, homophobia is well established on reservations among more acculturated/assimilated tribal people.[17] For example, many assimilated Natives have replaced tribal specific names for men who have alternative sexual orientations with "faggot," "pervert," or "homo."[18] Melvin Harrison, director of the Navajo Nation AIDS Network, noted that the "Navajo Nation is generally homophobic . . . but there are places on the reservation where this is not so, especially among the traditional elders, but among younger people there is a lot of ridicule and intimidation and there have been some reports of violence against gay men."[19] Violence against two-spirit men has been documented on the Pine Ridge Reservation as well as others, some cases involving murder.[20] The increasing homophobia on reservations places many two-spirit men in danger of HIV/AIDS because the association of HIV/AIDS with homosexual behavior hinders some from getting tested. In addition to their own personal concerns, two-spirits fear that their families will be shunned by community members.[21]

Tribal communities and individuals have responded in a variety of ways to two-spirit men, particularly those with the HIV/AIDS infection. One recommendation was to "quarantine all those infected, test everyone for HIV antibodies, and run infected individuals off the reservation at gun point."[22] Another suggestion was that Native men with HIV/AIDS be "expelled from the reservation and sent back to the city to die alone in the cities without help, love and affection."[23] One two-spirit man speaking about his experience told how in his isolated tribal community he was asked to remove his niece, who lived with him, from the Head Start Program because they believed she could pass the disease to other children even though he was the one infected.[24]

Although these incidents occurred during the early stages of the HIV/AIDS epidemic, today tribes still tend to shy away from the needs of two-spirit men. The National Native American AIDS Prevention Center (NNAAPC) noted in 1996 that "over the seven years, among more than 300 individuals who have completed the training [HIV/AIDS], no more than three small groups chose to target gay/bisexual men . . . and when questioned . . . they would commonly say 'we don't know of any people like that in our community' or 'I would not be comfortable working with any men because of my religious beliefs.'"[25] In contrast, Charon Asetoyer, director of a Native health center, argues that the attitude on the Yankton Sioux Reservation has changed for the better. She believes that the Native community is showing more compassion and understanding and that it is the attitude in the Indian Health Service IHS that is problematic. She feels that the IHS health care providers are openly saying that they don't want to deal with people with HIV and feel that they should not have to.[26] The lack of interest in working with the most seriously affected HIV/AIDS target population, two-spirits, demonstrates that many individuals on reservations are not aware of the historical role of two-spirits, and do not understand the detrimental impact of Christian morality on tribal traditions.

Lack of understanding and discriminatory treatment of two-spirit men creates an environment where HIV/AIDS can spread unimpeded. Discrimination against two-spirit men discourages them from seeking medical services, especially where there are concerns about personal treatment and confidentiality on the part of the IHS. Melvin Harrison, director of the Navajo Nation AIDS Network, has found that on the Navajo Reservation people with AIDS will "test" the service before deciding to seek services in order to keep their status confidential. Charon Asetoyer has found several breeches in IHS confidentiality, and her center has supplied transportation to other testing sites or to other states to get HIV testing done.[27] If people do not trust the confidentiality of the reservation health services, the alternative is to seek medical services off the reservation. However, IHS will not pay for medical care off the reservation unless they refer clients to the facility.[28] This can place people with AIDS in dire financial straits or in danger of not receiving care at all.

The lack of HIV/AIDS education, prevention, and quality care on reservations has encouraged many Natives to migrate from reservations to urban areas. According to census data, 0.4 percent of Native people lived in urban areas in 1900. By 1990 the figure had risen to 56.2 percent.[29] The move from rural to urban settings in the twentieth century was influenced by government policies, wars, and economics. The United States Indian policies have always been geared toward assimilation and acculturation, and part of these policies included enticing tribal people to leave their homeland and move into cities to become part of the "dominant society." One such policy was the Relocation Program of the 1950s, whereby tribal people were assisted by the federal government to relocate from reservations to major cities. World War I and II also influenced the migration from rural to urban locations. As Native men and women joined the war effort, they were exposed to new places, experiences, and more economic opportunities, which lured them to the cities permanently. Economics was another major factor in the move from reservation to urban areas. This is not surprising since reservations, in general, have high unemployment rates, and "80 percent of the men may be chronically unemployed."[30]

Additional motives for two-spirit men to move into urban areas are the escape from discrimination on reservations and self-preservation. According to Ron Rowell, two-spirits "migrate to large cities . . . in order to live more openly or to find personal and professional opportunity."[31] Native writer Beatrice Medicine suggests that many tribal homosexuals have moved to San Francisco in an effort to remove themselves from the "sexual repression they often find on reservations."[32] Like other gay men from rural areas, Native men migrate to cities such as San Francisco, California, to be able to come out of the closet and "get in touch with their suppressed sexual feelings."[33]

San Francisco is an area that is considered "a haven for gay persons . . . attracting thousands of gay men and women from other areas of the country and the world" and an area that contains the "highest concentration of gay persons of any major city in the U.S."[34] It is also one of the top metropolitan areas with large numbers of Native Americans. California's Native population is over 90 percent urban, and the state has the second largest Native population of all states.[35] Besides containing large numbers of gays, San Francisco also has high rates of AIDS cases. For example, AIDS was the fourteenth leading cause of death overall in the United States in 1997, the eighth leading cause in California in 1996, and in San Francisco the leading cause of death among men in 1996.[36] Many two-spirits live in California. A 1995 census update noted that California's Native population was merely 12 percent, yet the state had 25 percent of all U.S. Native American AIDS cases through 1997.

As two-spirit men, particularly those who have been oppressed on the reservation, move into urban communities, they may feel sexually liberated and at times may engage in high-risk behavior. Some have argued, and I agree, that homophobia has advanced the AIDS epidemic because gay men are forced to satisfy their needs for intimacy in "unsafe settings: thus, commitment to monogamous and enduring relationships is made difficult and casual sex became widespread."[37] A study of HIV/AIDS among Navajos noted that urbanization "weakened the hold of traditional social norms and lessened the closeness of the sexual network. Thus, what was previously a closed, predictable network of sexual partners multiplied . . . and became an open, opportunistic network of known and unknown, Navajo and non-Navajo, sexual partners."[38]

The rural-urban circular migration found among the Navajos is common among many urban Natives who return frequently to the reservation for ceremonies, seasonal activities, family gatherings, and funerals. Stephen, who found support for his HIV status among his tribe, finds it necessary to move to and from the reservation in search of continued support, healing, and fun. Many who are familiar with this migration phenomenon fear its possible contribution to the spread of HIV/AIDS because high-risk behavior outside the reservation will then expose rural partners. Melvin Harrison has observed that many bisexual men go to urban areas to have sex with other men and then return to the reservation. This action, he believes, seriously impacts the Navajo reservation because "Navajos are now infecting other Navajos [with AIDS]."[39] The possibility of two-spirit men infecting rural residents is based on the fact that the majority of HIV/AIDS infected Natives are urban. A recent Centers for Disease Control and Prevention (CDC) report was misleading because it stated that the "Native AIDS epidemic was predominantly a rural and Western phenomenon," NNAAPC countered that "actual data in the report show that sixty-eight percent of Native AIDS cases are reported in cities with populations of over 500,000."[40] The fear is not that urban HIV-infected people are consciously infecting others, but that "HIV-infected individuals do not know it [their positive status] and continue living their lives as they always have," and may contribute to the spread of HIV/AIDS.[41] It is important for both urban and rural individuals to be responsible, informed, and safe.

Once two-spirit men relocate to urban areas, it does not mean they are free of problems. The adjustment from a reservation to an urban setting varies from person to person but is likely to be difficult. Like other marginalized people in the United States, Natives are "at risk for high rates of mental disorders, alcoholism, suicide, and other disorders that are associated with high rates of social stress."[42] Two-spirit men who move to the city frequently have difficulties finding employment, and thus poverty, homelessness, and substance abuse may become integral parts of their lives.[43] Tom, whose story was discussed at the beginning of the chapter, found San Francisco a positive experience based on his sexual orientation, but at the same time, his drug abuse and criminal record led him to a life of deepening poverty and homelessness. This type of situation contributes to feelings of hopelessness and uncertainty for many urban Natives, and when combined with a diagnosis of HIV/AIDS, it can be overwhelming. Jodi Harry, a Miwok living in San Francisco who was diagnosed with AIDS in 1987, immediately committed suicide after his diagnosis.[44] To many two-spirit men his suicide was a wake-up call to the fact that AIDS was not just a white gay man's disease and that more support was needed. Curtis Harris, who worked for the American Indian Community House (AICH) as a health representative, noted a need in New York for culturally appropriate HIV/AIDS education and services. He founded AICH's HIV/AIDS Project in the late 1980s.[45] Sadly, culturally appropriate services do not necessarily stop the depression attached to a diagnosis of HIV. In New York City, with a high percentage of urban Natives, four individuals committed suicide in 1993 after being diagnosed with HIV.[46] Suicide is thus one of several responses to an HIV positive diagnosis.

Jordan and Stephen spoke in their interviews about the difficulty of telling people about having HIV/AIDS. Another HIV-infected man compared telling about his positive diagnosis to "coming out," and was concerned about the "impacts upon his friends, family, community members, and job" when he told them.[47] Those with an HIV diagnosis must learn to accept their precarious health status and the reality that they are living with a transmittable and stigmatized virus. They face great difficulty having to adjust to the onset of sickness and the idea of eventual death, as well as contending with changes in their identities (healthy man versus diseased man) and lifestyles.[48] A Sioux man spoke of how after diagnosis "life as he knew it ended."[49] An HIV diagnosis places Native people, still experiencing the effects of European colonization – loss of land, language, and family – at further risk of posttraumatic stress syndrome, depression, and other psychiatric disorders, as well as alcoholism.[50]

One aspect of the urban lifestyle that places both white gay men and two-spirit men at great risk for the HIV infection is the "bar scene." In urban bars men can freely meet other men with a similar sexual orientation. San Francisco, for example, has bar establishments that cater to specific populations, including two-spirit men.[51] Some two-spirit men have stated that the bar scene and sex are the only things that give their lives meaning.[52] The problem is that the bar scene is highly sex charged and focuses on alcohol, setting the stage for sex while intoxicated. Researchers have found that "men who meet their sexual partners in a bar are more likely to engage in unsafe sex."[53] Unsafe sex under such conditions is reported by many two-spirit men. One acknowledged that when he worked in a bathhouse in San Francisco he "often had sex while in an alcoholic blackout."[54] Public health officials and some gay community members have been attempting to shut down bathhouses because they are viewed as places where "anonymous sex with multiple partners occur."[55]

The Friendship House Association of American Indians, a drug and alcohol treatment facility in San Francisco, has found that the majority of the Native two-spirit men they serve are alcoholics, and many engage in unprotected sex while under the influence. Many of their clientele also lived on the street as indigents, worked as prostitutes, and had multiple sexual partners. The Friendship House found that two-spirit men are at furthe risk because they are often unable to change their sexual practices, feeling a sense of powerlessness and victimization that stems from a variety of early childhood experiences, which may include physical abuse.[56] In an effort to confront the issues facing two-spirit men, the Friendship House has incorporated a holistic approach to alcohol and substance abuse recovery, and includes HIV/AIDS prevention in the recovery curriculum. They have trained clinical staff in HIV/AIDS prevention and intervention and require all clients to participate in HIV/AIDS education during their recovery program.

The Indian Friendship House is an urban facility that tribal people will use, in part, because of its cultural orientation and services. Like other minority gay men, Native urban two-spirit men have been a subpopulation that is hard to reach and service. In part, their inaccessibility derives from feelings of being targets of racism, prejudice, and alienation in a white world. It has been determined that many two-spirits will not seek HIV/AIDS services from agencies that primarily serve white gay males, and when they do they still face problems.[57] For instance, Willie, a Native American attorney with AIDS who lives in San Francisco, complained about social workers in the city. He felt that they need to be more concerned about two-spirit conditions and that they "were not always available – they would cancel appointments, and have him wait long periods before seeing them. . . . He felt that many times he did not have the strength to ride around on public transportation going to appointments that were canceled or wait long periods and . . . [that] what was needed was more compassion for the various conditions of those who are HIV/AIDS infected."[58]

In contrast to the situation described by Willie, agencies such as the Urban Indian Health Board's Native American Health Center in San Francisco have been praised by those who utilize them. Developed through the urging of the American Indian community in the San Francisco and Bay Area, the center was opened in 1972 and today has two fully staffed clinics, one in San Francisco and the other in Oakland, California. In 1994 the center started the Native American AIDS Project (NAAP), which provides culturally sensitive HIV prevention and care to Natives in San Francisco. NAAP embraces the entire community of men and women, whether gay or straight, sober or substances abusers. The majority of NAAP's clients are unemployed or make less than eleven thousand dollars per year, and are males who have had substance abuse issues.[59] The director of NAAP, Joan Benoit, noted that the project does lots of street outreach to garner "the voices and people that are hard to reach."[60] To communicate HIV prevention messages and provide care to HIV/AIDS positive clients, project coordinators utilize Native cultural, spiritual, behavioral, and medicinal traditions. Recently they have added traditional healers to their project and believe it is the most powerful component. They are looking for more healers to participate in this program.

It is critical to take into consideration an individual's culture in prevention and care. Two-spirits have been known to refuse conventional medical and social services because they had previously been treated poorly due to their race, sexual preferences, and/or HIV/AIDS status. Care of those with HIV/AIDS is becoming a major concern at the beginning of the new millennium. With the onset of "cocktail" treatments HIV individuals are living longer lives, which means that providing quality medical care for them can become an immense challenge. Adding to the challenge is that many non-Native professionals are insensitive to Native cultural issues and do not permit traditional spiritual practices in their facilities.[61] For example, Curtis Harris, director of the American Indian Community House HIV/AIDS Project in New York City, was lectured by a nurse for burning sweet grass in a hospital room.[62] Sweetgrass is used by many tribal people for purification and healing. Thus facilities, services, and outreach that are not geared toward the needs of two-spirit men can result in the continuing spread of HIV/AIDS within that subtarget population.

Other barriers to effective HIV/AIDS health education, care, and access for two-spirits arise from political circumstances. It has proven difficult for many mixed-bloods to access the urban Indian Health Service because they do not have the required proof of tribal enrollment, leading them to depend on Medicare or Medicaid, neither of which provides culturally sensitive services.[63] Concern over meeting federal requirements to be eligible for health care was raised by Michael White Bear Claw (Cheyenne), a member of the Los Angeles County Commission on HIV Health Services. According to him, a high percentage of the California tribes are not federally recognized.[64] Natives living in New York City have also addressed the issue of identity and in a 1994 report recommended that the state "stop telling them who is or is not an Indian."[65] They also urged tribal people to decolonize their minds and to reevaluate who a Native American is because too many people are falling through the cracks due to their inability to verify their Native identity.[66]

Another problem that urban two-spirit men face in accessing health services is the lack of urban Indian health services. The presence of urban IHS is meager because it receives only 1.2 percent of the IHS annual budget to support a network of thirty-four urban clinics.[67] Even more disheartening is the fact that in Southern California, where there are an estimated two hundred thousand Native people, there is "no Indian clinic to offer treatment of services for our [Native] people living with the AIDS or HIV virus."[68]

Money is another serious barrier to effective HIV/AIDS health education and care. Allocation of funding determines what studies will be done. Federal funding has seldom been allocated to the study of HIV/AIDS among Native people because of their low AIDS prevalence rates. Funding also determines types of services offered, and once again, Native funding is frequently lacking. Governmental funding generally "goes where the disease is," and it is not aimed at prevention. For example, more money is needed for HIV testing for two-spirit men because they can unknowingly pass the infection on if they are not aware they are infected. Not knowing they are infected can also quicken the progression of HIV to AIDS because they do not access the appropriate health care. Of the thirty-four urban IHS clinics in the United States, only four provide HIV testing or HIV/AIDS case management services.[69] The American Indian AIDS Institute in San Francisco noted that "one deterrent to testing was that none of the nine anonymous testing sites in San Francisco employed a Native pre- and post-test counselor."[70] There is clearly a need for more testing of two-spirit men as well as the hiring of culturally competent or aware individuals to staff the testing sites.

Some barriers to appropriate prevention and care are internal to Native societies. One internal barrier to effective HIV/AIDS prevention among two-spirit men is the inability of people in tribal communities to discuss sex and sexual behavior. In general, tribal communities have accepted various types of gender and sexual orientations, but it is not something that is "openly" talked about. Terry Tafoya, a Native AIDS activist, has noted that some tribal educators "have been asked to not talk about sex" but he also notes that "sometimes we [tribal educators/communities] can not afford that luxury any longer."[71] The idea that sex should not be discussed is changing due to the efforts of many AIDS activists, health workers, and tribal communities.

Finding the correct and appropriate way to discuss HIV/AIDS prevention can be a daunting task for many reasons. In some cases language is a barrier. In Alaska, for example, an AIDS educator had difficulty finding a Yupik word for condom and eventually called upon the Yupik community to develop a word for it.[72] In this case the AIDS prevention specialist chose the best approach: to involve the community in finding culturally appropriate ways to discuss issues around HIV/AIDS.

Understanding the community is critical for effective HIV/AIDS intervention and prevention. Native organizations, AIDS agencies, and university researchers use a variety of methods and recommendations for conducting community assessments. The National Native American AIDS Prevention organization helps tribes conduct need assessments. The Tri-Ethnic Center for Prevention Research at Colorado State University has developed a model for assessing community needs for alcohol and drug abuse prevention. They have recently revised their Community Readiness Model, which was specifically developed for alcohol and drug abuse prevention, to assess Native community readiness in regard to HIV/AIDS prevention. Presently they are engaged in community readiness and HIV/AIDS prevention assessments in rural America. These assessments explore Native community attitudes about HIV/AIDS, community and cultural beliefs about the problem, the terms used by men and women to discuss HIV/AIDS issues, and beliefs about appropriate and inappropriate interventions. They are analyzing the data collected from community readiness assessments to develop culturally appropriate materials and prevention and intervention approaches.

Many health and tribal officials, AIDS activists, and organizations point out that prior to approaching Native communities about HIV/AIDS prevention speaking to the elders is crucial. In tribal communities, elders are gatekeepers of culture and tribal lifeways and their support in prevention is essential. Thus it is important for health workers to get the support of the elders because their cooperation makes their work more acceptable, and programs will work more smoothly. Many tribal communities follow the lead of their elders and respect their insights and guidance.

In the *American Indians Against HIV/AIDS Leadership Project* video, Carole LaFavor stresses that tribal elders must be involved in the fight against HIV/AIDS and describes how she always meets with them and asks them to have patience with her while she talks about sexual behaviors and habits.[73] In another Leadership Project video, Martin Broken Leg, a Native Episcopalian priest, professor, and AIDS activist, argues that "Native taboo topics" must be addressed in an effort to effectively deal with AIDS. He talks about how in the old days tribal communities did not talk about such things, but "to survive we have to talk about HIV/AIDS."[74] Earl Pike, an HIV/AIDS consultant, confirms that many Native people have grown up in a world where the discussion of sex was largely taboo and that those messages "are deep and powerful" and hard to overturn. Yet, to be an effective HIV/AIDS educator, Pike argues that they must speak openly and honestly and not "stay behind safe boundaries of discussion where no embarrassment is possible."[75]

In conjunction with being culturally sensitive about HIV/AIDS and sexual topics, more open discussions about sex and more studies on Native Americans and sexual behavior are called for. Terry Tafoya (Taos Pueblo) deems these things important because he believes that sexual behavior cannot be changed if it is not understood.[76] The issue of understanding sexual behavior is significant because most HIV/AIDS is transmitted through sex. Tafoya's call is also important because HIV/AIDS transmission is tied to how individuals perceive risk. Many have argued that education is not enough to change sexual behavior and that what is needed is a fuller understanding of why individuals place themselves in risky situations.[77]

The perceptions of risk are closely tied to personal ideas about HIV/AIDS. The beliefs that AIDS is a gay white man's disease and that AIDS happens to somebody else are obvious barriers to sexual behavior modification. The concept of AIDS being a white man's disease is prevalent throughout Indian country, as well as urban areas, and is a misconception that many tribal agencies are trying to address through HIV/AIDS education. Moreover, the idea that AIDS happens to somebody else [younger gay men], has been shown to be prevalent among older gay men who feel they have already gone through the AIDS epidemic.

Older gay men have been found to be at risk due to their preconceived notions about HIV/AIDS and the preconceived notions held by health workers. Many in the health profession perceive older gay men as no longer engaging in sex or being involved in substance abuse, and thus no longer vulnerable to HIV.[78] This notion is held by health officials, in part, because older gay men, those who are fifty years of age or older, do not disclose their sexual orientation, live secretive lives, and often have internalized society's homophobia.[79] The combination of society's misunderstanding of older gay men, the men's reluctance to disclose their sexual behavior, and the belief that they are invulnerable leads to a dangerous situation. It places them, as well as their partners, at great risk because they do not seek out HIV/AIDS education or services.

Studies have shown that prevention programs for older gay men must be different from those for young gay men. It has been appropriately suggested that "survival during the AIDS era is no longer about starting to have safe sex; it is about maintaining safe sex."[80] Recent studies suggest that sexual behavioral changes are being adhered to by neither older men or adolescents.[81] As we move into the twenty-first century, prevention materials must address a complex and changing gay culture and stress the maintenance of safe sex. It is reasonable to assume that many of the characteristics and actions of older gay men are applicable to the actions of some two-spirit men, suggesting that Native AIDS organizations and health care professionals need to address the specific needs of both older and younger two-spirits.

The development of appropriate prevention messages is necessary to halt the spread of HIV/AIDS. As many have suggested, prevention messages must change with the times and realistically acknowledge the complex circumstances, such as intimacy and death, facing gay men. Walt Odets's recent article in the AIDS and Public Policy Journal calls for a more truthful and changing prevention message. He strongly believes that the mere message of safe sex is rote and that "rote guidelines are disempowering and promote discouragement, hopelessness, and the sense that inevitably one is going to 'make a mistake' and contract HIV." He argues that "it cannot be the foundation of education that serves a lifetime." [82] Odets and others promote prevention messages that include information such as "it is unprotected sex, not the number of sexual partners or sexual orientation . . . that constitutes risk" and that "it is sometimes quite safe to have ordinary sex." [83] More truthful messages, Odets believes, will help men "develop the access to information and judgment that would allow them to make the best decisions reflective of their values and their appraisals of acceptable risk [and he notes that] it is *possibilities*, not restrictions, that motivate a man to take care of his health." [84]

Two-spirit men encounter several barriers to HIV/AIDS care, assistance, and education, but these are not insurmountable, particularly when two-spirit men themselves are making efforts to empower themselves and their communities. Self-empowerment can be seen in the rise of organizations and gatherings that specifically address their place in society. One of the most powerful groups is the Two-Spirit Society of Colorado. During a recent conversation with a participant, David Young, I was very impressed with the work of this group. I was told that the Two-Spirit Society has been in its zenith the last couple of years. They have no officers and no formal meetings. This group comes together to pray, run ceremonies, and drum. They gather yearly for about ten days at a camp where "healing takes place – healing from disease, Christianity, and war mentality." The camp has no amenities and ceremony is practiced. The participants are taught the ancient way to "look at the world and live in the world," which entails self-respect and knowing and supporting the two-spirit place in the circle of life. No sex, drugs, or alcohol are allowed in the camp. Two-spirits from Canada and across the United States participate in this healing event. Taking care of themselves and their community, as well as understanding the ways of the ancestors, are essential to this group. As Young noted, "HIV rates [and their rise] in Native communities are reflective of the imposition of Christianity." He believes that traditional communities have all the tools necessary to take care of themselves but Christianity, in many ways, has broken some of the circles that enabled tribal people to care for themselves and others. His group pushes for the reinstatement of traditional values of caring for each other. Through this work he believes Natives will be better prepared to address the problems of HIV/AIDS.[85]

As two-spirits struggle with their special needs, they are being assisted by many Native AIDS organizations. One of the most effective is the NNAAPC in Oakland, California. NNAAPC is actively serving two-spirits and has targeted them for education, health care, and prevention efforts.

NNAAPC is a nonprofit corporation founded in 1987 in response to the lack of Native health agencies engaged in the work of HIV/AIDS among Native Americans. In 1988 it received its first funding award from the CDC. The main office is located in Oakland, California. The organization is governed by an all-Native board of directors that includes HIV-infected individuals, tribal officials, public health professionals, health care providers, and substance abuse program administrators. The mission of NNAAPC is to stop the spread of HIV and related diseases and improve the quality of life for members of Native communities infected and affected by HIV/AIDS. In sum, their purpose is to provide resources to Native communities and to support community efforts by providing education and information services, training, and technical assistance and offering case management and client advocacy services to Natives with HIV/AIDS. NNAAPC continues to be funded by CDC as well as by the Health Resources and Services Administration, the Ford Foundation, the Gill Foundation, the Silva-Moonwalk Fund, and various corporate donors.

NNAAPC's prevention services include providing technical assistance and training to Native American organizations, agencies, and communities; developing and disseminating publications; a Native American AIDS information line; and maintenance of a national database of Native-specific HIV information. Technical assistance includes targeted individualized assistance to aid Native communities in developing successful HIV/AIDS prevention programs. NNAAPC also provides consultation on program development, need assessments, and leadership development. Training is offered through annual and semi-annual regional workshops. They will also address specific needs of tribes and agencies and provide specialized training workshops. NNAAPC publications include a newsletter, *In The Wind*, and a journal, *Seasons*. Publications are offered through their toll free, twenty-four-hour, fax-on-demand service. Also available are articles, statistics, and other AIDS resources, such as videos.

A recent program emphasis at NNAAPC is their National Native American HIV/AIDS Client Database.[86] The database is a repository of data profiling Native American HIV/AIDS clients. Anyone can contribute to the database and the program contribution does not have to be a formal part of the NNAAPC case management network. They see the database as their strongest policy tool, and encourage submission of any information. Currently, nearly six hundred individuals have been documented in the database, representing seventy-two tribes. The identified risk categories in the database are dominated by men having sex with men.[87]

Tied to the client database and prevention services is NNAAPC's Research and Evaluation Division, which develops, implements, and analyzes data received from its programs. This division is also responsible for developing research projects that improve understanding and enhance the delivery of HIV/AIDS services as well as the quality of life for people living with the disease. Division personnel also participate in national dialogues for research in and among Native communities.

Understanding the importance of good strategic planning, NNAAPC has a Public Policy Division with an office in Washington DC to address national concerns related to HIV and to provide technical assistance to communities dealing with local policy issues. NNAAPC's public policy priorities for years 1999–2000, identified by their National Policy Advisory Council, and presented at the 1998 National Native American HIV/AIDS conference in Minnesota, include improving disease surveillance in the United States, ensuring availability of and access to AIDS drugs for Natives living with HIV/AIDS, ensuring Native coverage in the reauthorization of the Ryan White CARE Act, and educating tribal officials concerning the cost of treating HIV/AIDS.[88]

Another large component of NNAAPC is its client services. Part of the Native Care HIV/AIDS Integrated Services Network is a joint effort between NNAAPC, the Ahalaya Native Care Center, and six other Native organizations. All Network participants implement the Ahalaya Case Management Model to provide culturally responsive HIV/AIDS case management services and HIV education to local Native communities.

The Ahalaya Native Care Center, which began as the Ahalaya Project (Choctaw word for "to care for deeply"), whose main office is in Oklahoma City, started in 1991. The project was a branch of NNAAPC and became an independent subcontractor in March 2000. The Ahalaya Native Care Center serves HIV-infected Native Americans living in Oklahoma. The project provides case management for HIV/AIDS infected Native Americans working in collaboration with various local service providers to meet individual clients' needs. Case management services include health maintenance (i.e., support groups, hospitalization, and mental health counseling); practical support services (home health care, transportation, and day care); and specific Native services (Native American spirituality, traditional healing, and cultural awareness). The case management is funded through a variety of sources including the Special Projects of National Significance Program of the Health Resources and Services Administration, the Centers for Disease Control, and the National Institute of Health.

NNAAPC, whose inception was a response to the lack of services for urban two-spirit men, has expanded its work to include all subtarget populations, policy work, and publications. As the most prominent Native AIDS agency, it has met with tremendous success in both urban and reservation communities, because of its dedication, hard work, and compassion, as well as its interagency, intertribal, intergovernmental coordination and sharing of work and information. With the work of NNAAPC and other Native AIDS organizations, tribal communities are taking a lead in combating HIV/AIDS among Native Americans.

As the first documented group of infected Natives and those with the highest rates, two-spirits are confronted with a variety of challenges in the fight against AIDS. In many circumstances they have been blamed for their personal actions and infections. In examining the rise of HIV/AIDS among two-spirits, this chapter looked at how colonization and the imposition of Christianity changed the place and role of two-spirits in Native societies. Their place was demeaned and devalued. Many were forced to move off the reservation and into urban areas where they could live their lives more freely. The economic position of tribal people also made it necessary for many to move to the cities in search of a better life. As indicated by the personal interviews and studies of urban two-spirits, life in the city did not uplift their lives. To the contrary, many found discrimination, racism, poverty, and HIV/AIDS. Two-spirit men continue to face a challenge as they struggle to survival in a society that places them "at the bottom." But, as examples of self-determination, organizations such as NNAAPC can be models for medical self-sufficiency among family and community members. Other groups, such as the Two-Spirit Society of Colorado, have enabled two-spirits to regain their ancient ways of healing and nurturing. It is these self- and community-empowerment groups and agencies that will not only ensure that two-spirit men obtain high quality and effective HIV/AIDS services, but will assist in reviving respect for two-spirit people.

# NATIVE AMERICAN WOMEN
# AND HIV/AIDS  *Those Who Bring Forth Life*

1 **2** 3 4

As a Native American woman and mother of a young teenage daughter, I have become personally concerned about the increase of HIV among Native women and adolescents. My personal interest in stopping the spread of HIV/AIDS is also driven by my life experiences. I was raised in a low socio-economic class that led me to poor life choices and high-risk behaviors. I no longer live that life and now make healthy choices, but I consider myself fortunate that I can. I know well the difficulties of rising out of poverty and understand many of the social structures that can hamper or help the process. I also understand that many do not rise out of poverty and it is not always due to the lack of trying but to the social structures that make the move impossible. It is within these structures that HIV/AIDS can flourish.

I begin this chapter with the stories of three women: Debi, Regina, and Sally. These women are from different tribes but are tied together in their struggle to survive in a society where they are "at the bottom" socially and economically. This situation, common to many women, has led these women to unhealthy life choices and to their infections. Their stories will speak to many of the issues raised in this chapter.

DEBI

Debi was born on a reservation in North Dakota, and her family moved to San Francisco in the 1960s as part of the Relocation Program. The move was difficult for her because her family was placed in a predominately African American community, and Debi was not familiar with other races. She has lived in San Francisco ever since but returns to the reservation regularly.

Although her family relocated to the city in hopes of pulling out of poverty, they did not succeed. Both of Debi's parents were alcoholics, and shortly after their relocation they separated. At that point Debi's mother took the kids back to the reservation, where she continued to drink. One day her mother went into town and never came back. After their mother disappeared Debi and her older brother took care of their five younger siblings. It was three weeks before their aunt and grandmother discovered they were alone. Finally, their father returned and took them back to San Francisco to live. Debi and her two other sisters were raised for a while by their father and stepmother, but the other children ran away.

For Debi, life in the city with her father was hard. He drank heavily and began to physically abuse her stepmother. Because of the abuse Debi and her siblings were placed into foster and group homes. While in state custody Debi was moved to different foster and group homes. She finally ran away at age eleven and has basically been on her own since then.

Debi's life on the street was difficult, and to support herself she participated in prostitution, selling drugs, and doing anything to survive. She married a man for money and does not know whether that marriage was ever annulled. She had her first STD, gonorrhea, when she was fourteen years old – her father took her to a clinic for treatment. Around age fifteen she was arrested for armed robbery and was "locked up for two and a half years." After her release she married an abusive man who was an alcoholic, and soon her son was taken away from her by the state. At that point she began to drink more. Her marriage began to deteriorate and she divorced at age twenty-one. She then lived on the street for approximately ten years. She was in and out of jail at this time and notes, "half the time I was homeless." Most of the time she sold drugs, drank heavily, and engaged in prostitution.

While living on the streets, she was not aware of HIV, although she knew about syphilis, gonorrhea, and other STDs. It was not until the 1980s that she began to hear about HIV, and in response she "sometimes" used condoms with "tricks" but did not use them with her "boyfriends." She had a variety of boyfriends in the next few years and most of them were abusive. Some were Native and all were drinkers. After a number of sexual encounters with one of her boyfriends, he informed her that he was HIV positive. Debi was briefly upset that he did not tell her of his HIV status, but at that time "she didn't give a shit" because she was living on the street "getting loaded every day . . . and basically living in blackouts." She also was in and out of the hospital for drug overdoses. Her drugs of choice were heroin and cocaine.

Today, Debi believes that "subconsciously she was trying to commit suicide" because six months after being with her HIV-positive boyfriend she found out that she too had the infection. At this point Debi had three children. Her daughter was raised mainly by her sister, and her third child was adopted by her cousin. Both were raised on the reservation. Her son was raised by foster parents in California.

She is now with a man she has known for several years, although they have had an on-and-off relationship. Debi infected him by having unprotected sex because she was afraid to tell him of her diagnosis, not because of violence, but because she was afraid he would leave her. He has remained with her.

At a time when Debi and her boyfriend were having difficulties, her sister returned her pregnant daughter to her because she could not control her. The HIV infection seemed minor compared to the other problems Debi began to face daily. When her daughter turned fifteen, Debi thought "Oh my God, what am I going to do now? I've got this disease, my daughter's pregnant, my sister can no longer deal with her, I have a drinking problem, and I am living in a hotel." Her life was extremely difficult at this time. Her daughter was unmanageable. She basically "wouldn't listen, ran away regularly, and did whatever she wanted." Debi felt, however, that her daughter needed her, so she worked on getting herself clean and sober. It was a difficult journey. She struggled to control her habits as well as her daughter's. Her daughter eventually gave birth but the child was taken away to be raised on the reservation. Her daughter then began to "work on the street, started doing crack, and got a pimp and everything else."

Debi and her daughter finally turned their lives around and for the last five years have been supportive of each other. Clean and sober, Debi became pregnant again and had a baby. Although she and her partner of nine years are HIV positive, the baby is negative. Debi continues to try to make healthy choices and stay clean, but finds it hard. She lives in the same neighborhood where she was using drugs and constantly walks by old friends and old places. But she endures.

She has traveled to and from the reservation and notes how the disease is there as well as in the city. But she feels that "tribal people, today, are more aware" of the disease, which is a good thing.

SALLY

Sally was born in Oregon to a tribe that was prosperous. The tribe, however, fell into despair and depression with the enactment of the federal Termination Policy. Both parents are Natives and early in her youth they moved to the Bay Area in California. Sally was never homeless. Although her parents smoked weed and crank and did heroin, they always had a home and she always had her own room. She joined her parents in taking drugs and she considers her downfall to have been her intravenous drug use.

Sally began to do intravenous drugs when she was sixteen. She started with crank, moved to heroin, and when she got tired of "being up," she began to use cocaine and speedballs (cocaine and heroin). Sally spoke of her mind being on only one thing – getting high. She did not have to have a reason to do drugs, she would "just do it."

Closely intertwined with Sally's drug use was crime. Sometimes she would commit crimes for drugs or the crime was related to drug use. This lifestyle combination led her to spending eighteen of her years "doing time, on and off." As we spoke, she considered herself as still doing time since she was on parole. She spoke of wanting "to do good and trying to do good."

Sally was diagnosed with HIV six years ago. Her drug habit was so serious that she was at the point where she would break her needle someplace and would have no money for another one, so she would "go to places where other people were fixing and use their needles." Her diagnosis was no shock to her or her family.

Sally told her family immediately about her HIV diagnosis and they were as supportive as they could be. She even began to be more cautious around family and friends and became "protective of the things" she used. In her early years she had no reservation because her tribe was terminated and was not reinstated for several years. She has today, however, become enrolled and is attempting to enroll her daughter. She feels that she and her daughter can have more support as enrolled tribal members.

Although she told her parents, she has not told her entire immediate family about her HIV status. The fathers of her children know, particularly the father of the child that she was carrying when she was diagnosed with HIV. The child was born negative and Sally immediately had her tubes tied so she could no longer have children. She does not want to burden her children with her HIV status. Of her three children, her oldest daughter, who is nineteen years old, is the only child aware of her status. Sally is cautious about whom she tells and she tells only those she thinks are "intelligent enough to handle it" and not those who can use it against her. In jail she had her status used against her. Other inmates would say that she tried to spit on them or bite them, which then led to charges. She finds not being able to tell people frustrating, which has forced her to keep to herself inside and outside prison.

Although Sally was HIV positive she continued to do drugs, but she was open with the people she did drugs with. She kept her own stuff and would tell them she had HIV. Some of her friends even "tried to get with her because they did not care" about her status but she would refuse. Because of her disease Sally is not looking for a relationship but is more interested in "just a hug, to be curled up and just talking and socializing." Sally would attend powwows and Indian gatherings as a form of socializing when she was young, but she no longer does so because she has bad memories of people attending them "just to get high." The Indian gatherings in Oklahoma, however, she found to be more traditional and without drugs and alcohol.

Sally was helped by her mother, as well as HIV-positive jail mates, in finding medical services for HIV. She has not found any problems of discrimination but, instead, favoritism. She felt that those who used services regularly received more attention and more assistance. She also felt that the HIV/AIDS service was better in San Francisco than in the surrounding areas.

As for her future, Sally is aware of the difficulties she faces in her life. What she is working toward is more control of herself and her life and "the building of a strong foundation." She thinks that she lacks a strong foundation because she spent too much of her life "doing time."


REGINA

Regina was born in Texas, a state that once had many tribal people who moved between Mexico and the United States. Today, however, Texas no longer has federally recognized tribes due to a variety of federal removal policies. Yet there are still a number of tribal communities. Regina was raised knowing very little of her heritage, but she knew she was Native and German. Being Native was not a positive attribute in Texas, and her father was disowned for not marrying "his own kind." He was also an alcoholic.

Regina married at the early age of seventeen to a mixed-blood and had two children. Her first child came one year after their marriage. Her other child was conceived through violence. At a keg party she was raped by one of her husband's friends. She did not tell her husband until she was six months pregnant. Her husband responded by physically abusing her, so they temporarily separated. When she was seven months pregnant Regina went to the hospital because of a severely abscessed tooth. At that point she began labor and "passed to the other side [died]." She said that she saw her grandparents, who told her that she needed to "forget everything that I had learned, that I had to learn a new way, and that I could not go any farther and had to go back." When she woke she had given birth to her daughter and was angry with the doctors for reviving her, because she was "happy over there."

Her husband began to do more and more drugs. Regina believed he treated her badly because of the rape. She also felt that he blamed her for the rape and thought that it was she who "had done something wrong in our relationship and that I wasn't good anymore." Her marriage remained difficult and relatives began to take care of her children. She finally divorced her husband, who by then was a habitual drug user and wife beater. Her second marriage, at the age of twenty-two, wasn't for love, but to help gain custody of her son. The judge ruled against Regina, stating that she could take care of two children but did not have enough income to take care of three. Regina was devastated at not regaining her son.

Regina's marriages were always troubled. Her first husband taught her how to "shoot up drugs" shortly after the birth of their first child. He was nine years older than Regina and had a tremendous amount of control over her. The second marriage, for convenience, did not work either. Since she did not regain custody of her children, she left her second husband. She began dating different men, and she believes that one of them gave her the HIV infection. Although Regina had been an intravenous drug user while she was with her first husband, she now believes she contracted the infection when she was twenty-three, around 1986.

After a car accident in the 1990s, Regina attempted to get her life together. She fell in love and married again in 1992. In 1993 she applied for health insurance. In order to qualify she had to get a physical and give a blood sample. Her HIV-positive result from her blood test came at a bad time – on the same day that her mother died. It was a difficult day and she felt "flipped out" and did not know whether to "cry for myself or to cry for my mother." Her drinking problem worsened once again.

She mourned for her mother, whom she had been very close to, and felt she was left to survive on her own. She continued to have problems with drinking and drugs, particularly since her husband refused to quit drinking. He would tell her that she had the problem, not him, and she was the one that needed to stop drinking. Her family and children found out about the diagnosis after she had an argument with her husband. The daughter and her friend overheard the conversation and passed the information to others. Her life got even worse after that. Her family and friends would not touch her, and she could not visit relatives because they did not want to put their "children in danger [of infection]." She eventually left her husband in Texas and came to California in 1995.

The move was not what she expected (she had hoped for a better life) and while living in Oakland she was introduced to crack and began to use it. The disease and the crack were "eating her up." She tried to keep her life together but found the struggle too difficult. She was doing crack while she was taking her AIDS medications. Eventually she became sick with pneumonia. While she was ill she gave her daughter to her son to take care of. He then refused to give her back. Regina's son is very angry with her because she has full-blown AIDS. AIDS is only one of many problems confronting Regina. She also has cancer.

Regina continues to strive for a better life against tremendous odds. She is no longer "doing drugs" while she takes her meds. She no longer drinks alcohol and would like to "educate people that it is okay to be around us [those infected], how we can be family members, and we can be productive members of society." But life still remains a struggle and Regina emphasizes that "HIV destroyed my marriage, family, kids, and my whole life" and that "I am alone because of HIV." Yet she is proud and happy to have the support of a Native agency for her medical, physical, and psychological needs.

The stories of Debi, Sally, and Regina are common among many disenfranchised and impoverished Native women. The mere fact that they were born into poverty put them, from the outset, at high risk for HIV/AIDS. Their stories show that the decisions they made were linked to economic, social, and at times, cultural processes. It is the social dynamics that led to the transmission of HIV to these and other women in this chapter.

The standing of women in traditional Native societies varied from tribe to tribe, but in many tribes women held positions of political, social, military, and spiritual leadership. They had the right to choose marriage partners, divorce, own land and property, as well as take up critical roles in trade, the home, acculturation, assimilation, and political activism. In sum, Native women had "egalitarian" roles within their societies. The role of Native women today remains vital in a variety of tribal communities. Recent studies emphasize that women form the "very core of indigenous resistance to genocide and colonization" and are essential in transmission of culture.[1] The most important role of Native women, however, continues to be the role of mother. To bear and/or care for Native children is a position of honor and value throughout Native North America. Hence, the health and well being of Native women is essential to the well being of all.

Although elements of women's traditional standing are found in the lives of many modern Native women, many things have changed. Native women today, like women in the United States in general, have less economic, social, and political power than men. They are often a silent and marginalized group, with many relegated to dependency upon male partners. In addition, as women of color, Native women have a lower status economically, educationally, and socially. Their position in society impacts every facet of their lives, particularly their health. The scope of this chapter covers the rise of AIDS among Native American women, their vulnerabilities, the activities that promote the spread of HIV, and what is being done in the area of prevention. Since there is very little information on Native women and HIV/AIDS, I have relied on research from the Native American Women's Resource Center in South Dakota as well as general research on women and AIDS. Research on women and AIDS is becoming more substantial as AIDS becomes increasingly heterosexually transmitted. It has been found that the women at most risk share the same low social and economic status as men. These findings are applicable to tribal women.

HIV/AIDS is one of the most dangerous health problems for poor women around the world. Women account for more than 40 percent of the thirty million people worldwide infected with HIV, and the majority are poor women.[2] This statistic places a new face on the disease, a woman's face.

HIV/AIDS was identified in women early in the epidemic but virtually ignored. When AIDS was first recognized among young gay men, the disease was also identified in a woman. Shortly thereafter, other cases were reported that included women who injected drugs, hemophiliacs, and the poor – groups that did not share the same risk factors as young gay men.[3] Yet AIDS continued, particularly in the United States, to be labeled a gay man's disease or, from a Native American perspective, a white gay man's disease. This misunderstanding and misinformation about HIV/AIDS, coupled with current news reports that the number of reported AIDS cases is decreasing, has led many to believe AIDS is no longer a problem and particularly not a woman's problem.

Contrary to the popular understanding of HIV/AIDS and its impact, statistics demonstrate that infection is growing rapidly among women. In the United States the proportion of AIDS cases among adult/adolescent women has increased from 7 percent of the annual total in 1985 to 17 percent in 1999.[4] Although infection among women has grown steadily, it was not until 1995 that the First National Scientific Meeting on HIV Infection in Adult and Adolescent Women was held in Washington DC.[5] The main theme of conference was that women have been silenced in the epidemic and given "seriously short shrift in AIDS research and treatment."[6] The participants noted that women were increasingly dying from AIDS and called for action.

While the number of women diagnosed with AIDS in the United States is steadily increasing, all women are not affected equally. Of the reported AIDS cases among women in 1999, African Americans represented 57.3 percent (71,089), whites 21.7 percent (26,960), Hispanics 19.9 percent (24,800), Asian/Pacific Islanders 0.5 percent (652), and Native Americans 0.2 percent (371).[7] The alarming statistics show that certain ethnic women represent large percentages of their respective ethnic group: African Americans

Fig 3. AIDS cases by gender and ethnicity

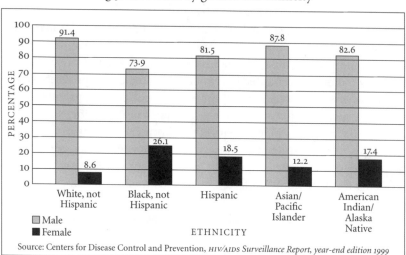

Source: Centers for Disease Control and Prevention, *HIV/AIDS Surveillance Report, year-end edition 1999*

26.1 percent, Hispanics 18.5 percent, Native Americans 17.4 percent, Asian/Pacific Islanders 12.2 percent, and whites 8.6 percent (fig 3).

Because the total number of Native AIDS cases is low, the threat to Native women has not been acknowledged until recently. Tribal communities are becoming more aware of the increase of HIV/AIDS among Native women, as indicated in their participation in such conferences as Empowerment: A Strategy for HIV/AIDS Prevention and Access to Care Among Women of Color and The Native Women and Wellness Conference in 1997.[8] Both conferences specifically addressed the wellness of Native women. Another indicator of concern over the rise of AIDS among Native women can be found in a recent headline in the *Navajo Times,* "WARNING! 3 pregnant Native Women test HIV positive." The article notes that "AIDS has no boundaries." It goes on to say that in the past ten years only two women were diagnosed with HIV on the Navajo Reservation, but "in the past six months three pregnant Native American women in the Navajo Area of Indian Health Services have tested positive for HIV."[9]

One factor that makes women more vulnerable to HIV infection today is the large number of men who have AIDS. In the United States more men (609,326) than women (124,045) have AIDS.[10] HIV cases reported through December 1999 from thirty-four areas with confidential reporting demonstrate that there are twice as many males with the HIV infection (88,400) as females (34,200).[11] The growing number of infected males increases the odds that a female will have an infected partner.

In spite of the larger number of infected males, HIV is considered by some scholars to be a "biologically sexist" disease in that women are biologically more susceptible.[12] Some studies show, for example, that because the virus is more concentrated in seminal fluids than in vaginal secretions, it is anywhere from two to twenty times more efficiently transmitted from men to women than from men to men.[13] Women are also more susceptible because HIV enters the bloodstream easily through the lining of the vagina and cervix.[14] Heterosexual transmission of HIV to women has risen from 13 percent of women with AIDS in 1983 to 39 percent in 1998.[15] Most alarming is the fact that women infected by heterosexual contact increased 243 percent from 1994 to 1998.[16]

Older women have additional risk factors. Some researchers argue that "vaginal dryness" and thinning of the vaginal wall are additional risk factors for some menopausal women because the increased susceptibility to tearing provides a pathway for HIV infection.[17] Research in the area of menopausal women and HIV/AIDS is notably lacking. The scant biomedical information on older women indicates that the disease may progress quicker in these women because of delayed diagnosis and/or immune suppression as a function of age. Also suggested in the literature is that "hormone replacement therapy may contribute to HIV risk through the immunodepressive effects of estrogen and progesterone."[18]

Women's vulnerability increases further when a sexually transmitted disease (STD) is present. The presence of STDs not only signifies high-risk behavior (i.e., unprotected sexual intercourse) but can assist in the transmission of HIV because STDs allow entry for HIV through open sores or microscopic breaks in affected tissue.[19] When a person is infected with a STD, "he/she is two to five times more likely to become infected with HIV."[20] The risk will vary depending on the particular STD. For example, ulcerative STDs carry the greatest risk because they affect the integrity of the vaginal protective barrier, creating an open portal of entry for HIV infection, and because they are host to the immune cells that HIV potentially infects.[21]

The relationship between HIV/AIDS and STDs place Native people in grave danger because Native communities have high STD rates. In South Dakota, for example, where Natives are 6.7 percent of the population, they represent 40.2 percent of the state's gonorrhea cases.[22] They have the highest gonorrhea percentage of any race in the state. A study of thirteen states revealed that gonorrhea and syphilis rates among Native people were twice that of non-Natives.[23] Chlamydia trachomatis, which has surpassed gonorrhea as the most common sexually transmitted disease in the United States with an estimated four million infections a year, is also a problem among the Native population.[24] The Indian Health Service is engaging in a campaign to stop the spread of chlamydia because Native communities have "the highest documented rates of chlamydia in the U.S."[25] A study in Alaska found that rates for rural Inupiat women were ten times higher than for the local non-Native population.[26] It is therefore easy to see why the IHS feels that the "prevention of STDs may be one of the most effective means to prevent HIV/AIDS."[27] The IHS statements are encouraging and echo calls for action by Native organizations. For several years the Native American Women's Health Education Resource Center has called for aggressive efforts to stem the STD rates in an effort to slow HIV transmission.[28] In addition, many women are exposed to the complications of undiagnosed or untreated STDS – 70 to 80 percent of STDS go unnoticed because individuals do not show any symptoms.[29] Furthermore, STDS such as chlamydia, gonorrhea, and primary syphilis may be asymptomatic, particularly in women. A screening of female patients in IHS facilities during routine pap smears found that 59 percent of chlamydia-infected women had no symptoms.[30] Thus, women may not even realize they are at higher risk for HIV infection.

STDS, like AIDS, tend to be diseases of poverty because they are intensified by conditions of economic hardship, whereby women do not have the money or time to get tested, hence their STD or HIV infection remains untreated. To many AIDS scholars and researchers, poverty is one of the leading co-factors in the advance of the global AIDS pandemic. This fact is distressing, especially for women, since 70 percent of the world's poor are women, hence at high risk.[31] Studies show that the HIV virus disproportionately affects women "from poor and minority populations in more affluent countries, and [who] come from a background of poor physical and mental health, malnutrition, and inadequate health care."[32] In the United States HIV has moved freely through impoverished communities. It has been suggested that collecting data on women and AIDS in the United States by ethnicity, rather than by socioeconomic status, distorts the fact that "the majority of women with AIDS in the U.S. are poor" and at extreme risk.[33]

Poverty prevents or inhibits people from obtaining health education, having access to good health care, and obtaining proper medical treatment – all of which assist in the prevention and treatment of AIDS. The low economic status for Native women thus places them in a potential high-risk category. In the United States the percentage of unemployment for females ages sixteen and older is 6.2 percent, but for Native women it is 13.4 percent.[34]

Utilizing a socioeconomic analysis, physician and AIDS activist Dr. Paul Farmer has found "that some women are, from the outset, at high risk of HIV infection, while other women are shielded from risk."[35] According to Farmer, women "whose social [and economic] status denies them access to the fruits of scientific and social advances" are made vulnerable to HIV/AIDS as a result of "structural violence."[36] His analysis shows that social processes shape the dynamics of HIV transmission and infection.[37] Debi, Sally, and Regina's stories address various types of social processes that have made it difficult for them to make positive changes, as well as the processes that have led to their infections.

With poverty comes a host of other factors, such as poor health, poor diet, and related diseases, that make Native people more vulnerable to HIV infection and to developing AIDS. Diabetes, a leading cause of morbidity and premature mortality in Native populations, weakens the immune system, hastening the progression of HIV to AIDS. The disease is widespread among tribal people and it has been found to be "a major threat to the health of indigenous people."[38] For instance, in the Aberdeen area of South Dakota, IHS statistics indicate that Native people with diabetes are "13 times more likely to require kidney dialysis, 6.5 times more likely to have lower extremities amputated, and half of those with diabetes will get diabetic eye disease that leads to blindness."[39] Diabetes as a co-factor in HIV/AIDS is especially relevant to women. A 1998 study reported that the majority of the 63,400 Native diabetics who received care from the Indian Health Service in 1996 were women.[40]

Since poverty is closely related to health and disease it is also a factor in determining the length of survival after developing AIDS. Survival studies indicate that women, in general, are more likely to die earlier than men once diagnosed with AIDS.[41] Some reports show that Native women follow this pattern. AIDS-related deaths, in general, dropped 26 percent between 1995 and 1996.[42] For Native people, between January 1996 and June 1996, AIDS deaths dropped by 32 percent when compared to January 1995 and June 1995. The decrease was more substantial among Native people than any other ethnic group and many credit the decline to an increase in access to care and improved treatment options accessed through Native American HIV case management programs. However, while Natives as a group experienced a decrease, women saw an increase of 3 percent in AIDS-related deaths.[43] There are several possible reasons for the rise in AIDS deaths among Native women. Survival studies have found that gender inequality (social and economic) may lead to the differences in survival rates.[44]

Researchers are not in complete agreement over why women die earlier.

Some researchers feel that survival differences may be due to biological factors. Others suggest that survival differences may have more to do with medical care because women tend to seek medical attention later, when their symptoms are already advanced, and then receive lower quality health care. This would be especially true for women who are heads of households and primary caretakers in families.[45]

According to the government census in 1997, 27 percent of the nation's American Indian family households were maintained by women with no husband present.[46] The difficulties that women who are heads of households encounter are enormous. As primary care givers many women must place their needs and concerns after the needs of their children and family. A recent study found that one-third of HIV patients forgo medical care because they can not afford the time or money.[47] They spend their money on basics such as food and shelter.

Like poor women in general, Native women have others dependent on them for essential needs. This is illustrated through the narrative of Nan, an HIV-positive forty-six-year-old Shawnee/Delaware woman with seven children. She explains that her number one need is to "make my bills meet at the end of each month and make sure my children are taken care of."[48] Sally also struggled with her infection as well as with taking care of her own daughter who was partaking in high-risk behaviors. Sally found it difficult to survive economically and turned to prostitution regularly. A woman who is HIV positive or has AIDS and is the head of the household is placed in an even more trying situation, with burdens of illness, emotional exhaustion, and the emotional needs of their own children. A recent study of HIV and family structure and the parenting challenges of HIV-infected mothers found that disclosure of their status to their children and planning for their children's future were the two critical issues facing them.[49] Between 1992 and 2002 an estimated 93,000 to 112,000 uninfected children will be born to infected women.[50] Neither Debi, Sally, or Regina had shared the news of their infections with all of their children for fear of rejection, as well as societal and tribal discrimination toward their children.

Another problem for poor women is obtaining adequate care even when medical care is available. Author Martha Ward has noted that poor women tend to receive inadequate health care in part because "service providers have a continuing orientation to middle class values."[51] Native women speak about the lack of compassion that health workers have for them and complain they are not viewed as "individuals."[52]

Another factor closely tied to receiving adequate care is isolation. One HIV-infected Native woman spoke of the hardship of getting "to places that know about HIV." She explained, "I live on a very limited income and I have to be very careful about my budget and try to make sure that I have enough money set aside for gas to get me to my doctor's appointment," seventy miles away.[53] Indeed, infected women who live in Indian country may have to travel as far as three hundred miles one way to a health clinic.[54] One Native woman described how she traveled on foot to a main road when her rural road was impassable and then hitchhiked to her doctor appointments.[55] According to Charon Asetoyer, director of the Native American Women's Health Center on the Yankton Sioux Reservation, transportation is a major problem in providing HIV/AIDS education, prevention, and intervention services. Asetoyer notes that first one must have a car, and then the car must be in good shape all year round to be able to get from point A to point B. Because many women do not have their own transportation or good transportation, the Women's Health Center provides transportation to women. The center transports people to Sioux Falls, Pierre, or to another reservation where they can get services or get tested.[56]

Powerlessness of Native women is another factor in potential HIV/AIDS infection, and it is also related to poverty. For example, poverty contributes to women's dependence and lack of power in the family, particularly if the partner is the one who "brings home the bread." Regina is a powerful example of a woman caught in that situation. Her husband was abusive and absolutely refused to wear condoms even when he knew that she was HIV positive. A sense of powerlessness limits the ability of women to insist on monogamous relationships or condom use, both of great importance in preventing the spread of HIV among women.

Condom use is one of the most effective means of preventing HIV transmission. Sadly, fewer than 20 percent of high school and college women who are sexually active use condoms, clearly indicating that new strategies are needed to prevent the spread of HIV.[57] Empowerment and effective communication are critical tools for women in condom negotiations. Condom use has been found to be a complex issue tied to poverty, self-esteem, preserving good family relations, physical abuse, rejection, and abandonment.[58]

Condom use is especially problematic for poor women in violent and abusive relationships. New studies are linking violence, poverty, and HIV risk.[59] Violent crime rates are highest for those whose annual income is less that $7,500.[60] A 2000 study suggested that women who reported a history of domestic violence were most likely over twenty-five years old, unemployed, not living with their spouse, and did not own their own home or apartment.[61] Studies have also shown that women who live in violent circumstances are too scared to demand that their abusive partners wear a condom. Women in the United States confront violence regularly. Statistics show that in their lifetime, fifty percent of women will be battered, with one out of three being physically abused repeatedly every year, and that every seventy-eight hours a women will be forcibly raped.[62]

The statistics for Native women are equally frightening. Although Native Americans comprise 0.6 percent of the U.S. population, 1.4 percent of victims of violence are Natives. Between 1992 and 1996 the rate of rape/sexual assault against Native people was 5.6 percent compared to the U.S. average of 4.3 percent.[63] The violent crime rate against Native females was 98 per 1,000 females, the highest among all female ethnic categories.[64]

In South Dakota, where Native women are a very small portion of the state population, they constitute 50 percent of the domestic violence shelter population.[65] In some areas abusive relationships for Native women are commonplace and limit healthy choices. Asetoyer, of the Native American Women's Health Center, believes that some women in abusive relationships are set up "for coming in contact with HIV." Many times the victim, Asetoyer states, "thinks she is in a monogamous relationship and does not realize that her abuser is out there screwing around and having relations with other women and men, and bringing home sexually transmitted diseases, and reproductive tract infections."[66]

A study of sixty-eight Native American women in New York City revealed that 44 percent reported a lifetime trauma that included domestic violence and physical or sexual assault.[67] Kashka, a Native Alaskan HIV-positive woman related, in an interview, that when her husband had sex with an HIV-positive male in the village, she was afraid to then ask him to wear a condom or refuse sex because it would make him "angry and violent." She also knew she would have little support from other women because she felt that in her village it was not right to refuse to have sex with one's husband.[68]

Along with producing what some clinicians call posttraumatic stress disorder in women, a history of childhood violence, and living with violence, makes negotiating safe sex extremely difficult.[69] Exposure to trauma and abuse among non-Native women has been associated with sexual risk behaviors. Many HIV-positive women have reported a history of abuse.[70] All three of my female interviewees were exposed to trauma and abuse when they were young, and they all engaged in high-risk behaviors at a very early age. A 2000 study strongly suggests that "domestic violence plays a significant role in the lives of women who are HIV infected . . . and abuse during childhood may lead to substance use, multiple sexual partners, and a lack of self-protection, which are all risk factors for HIV infection."[71] The study further reported that "women who have been abused as children also may be at greater risk for HIV infection."[72] It is likely that the abuse and trauma that Native women experience will also contribute to high risk HIV behaviors. The violence against Native women in the United States has become so severe that the federal government has recently published a Request for Proposals (1999) for studies on violence against Native women.

One topic that has been almost completely ignored is HIV/AIDS among lesbians. Lesbians are also at risk for HIV because violence against them is on the rise.[73] There is a general assumption that lesbians are immune from HIV/AIDS. This assumption has been perpetuated in part by medical researchers and clinicians, by the lack of national research, and by physicians who publicly declare that "lesbians don't have much sex."[74] It is generally believed that HIV transmission from female-to-female is minimal.[75] The CDC has actively chosen not to use a transmission category of women who have sex with women because they view it as a low-risk activity. This action silences and removes lesbians from the AIDS debate because CDC data assists in determining funding, hence, they are excluded from resources.[76]

Lesbians need a voice in the AIDS debate to keep themselves and their partners safe, as well as to carry out much-needed research and develop organizations that address the health needs of lesbians. Tara, a California native, lesbian, and AIDS activist who was diagnosed with AIDS in 1989 describes the difficulties she encountered when she was told of her diagnosis. There were no organizations for women with HIV/AIDS, and absolutely no services for lesbians. Tara's message in the late 1980s, that "none of us [lesbians] are just safe by virtue of our sexual identification or anything else," is still true today.[77] Many lesbians have come to realize that lesbianism is not a condom.

The assumption that lesbianism is a protection against HIV/AIDS gives the false message that lesbians have nothing to fear. The myth that the risk to lesbians is minimal does not take into consideration that lesbian sexual activities can be diverse. They may include bisexuality, sex work, and the use of sex toys that can potentially create tears that the HIV virus may enter through.[78] Studies of female-to-female transmission are critical for lesbians to adequately assess their risks and vulnerabilities to HIV.

Vulnerability for lesbians comes from the same sources as for other women, as well as from discrimination and the "gay lifestyle." Two surveys found that "the lesbian community is under-served, under-documented, and at greater risk than heterosexual women for a variety of health problems," because lesbians access health care less.[79] Lesbians do not access health care for a variety of reasons. Some report that they receive poor treatment because of their sexual orientation. In many instances they do not trust health services to provide them with adequate or quality care. Studies have reported that due to discrimination by society and health care personnel lesbians have high rates of breast cancer, are more likely to smoke, have a high prevalence of obesity, and high levels of stress.[80] In addition, for many Native lesbians the "coming-out" process is very difficult and some do so by immersing themselves in the white gay party scene, which places them at further risk.[81]

The issue of trust is vital for effective HIV/AIDS prevention and care for Native American women. A history of distrust for the government and health providers prohibits many Native women from seeking diagnosis, assistance, and medical attention. The distrust is a legacy of deliberately introduced diseases and sterilization abuse of Native women. Native American women were at least two times more likely to be surgically sterilized than other women of color and many were sterilized without informed consent.[82]

For many Native people mistrust is combined with a lack of confidence in the Indian Health Service. One problem is the issue of confidentiality in small, tight-knit Native communities where everybody knows everybody. Native women have described how they would "not even take brochures, fliers, or any HIV specific information for fear someone from the community might see it and guess about their HIV status."[83] There are others, however, who disagree with the idea that confidentiality is a problem. Gloria Bellymule, a Cheyenne RN and case manager, for instance, thinks that the confidentiality issue is "a lot of phobia, due to the close-knit nature of Native communities."[84]

Another problem is the lack of confidence that the IHS will provide appropriate and quality care. Cordelia Thomas, a forty-eight-year-old rural Oklahoma Native woman with AIDS complained that her health facility was ignorant about HIV/AIDS and that "it's hard for people in the rural areas to access help, get to places that know about HIV."[85] She further noted her disappointment in IHS because it had not prioritized HIV.

By far the factor placing women in most danger is behavior. For adult/adolescent women, the main behavioral risk is intravenous drug use, the source of 42 percent of all reported female AIDS cases through December 1999. In the heterosexual exposure category, over 40.7 percent of cases resulted from sex with an intravenous drug user. Native women have a higher percentage of intravenous drug use as a mode of transmission than any other race: 46 percent (fig. 4). Debi, Sally, and Regina participated in intravenous drug use and shared needles with many other users. At least two of them felt that this was the way in which they contracted the HIV infection.

Women who are intravenous drug users are placed at even greater risk by

Fig 4. Female adult/adolescent AIDS cases in intravenous drug use exposure category, by ethnicity

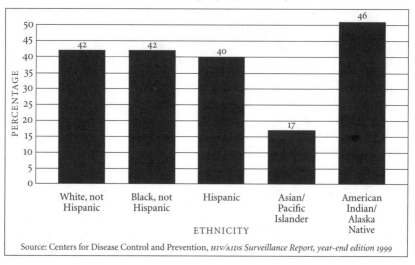

Source: Centers for Disease Control and Prevention, HIV/AIDS Surveillance Report, year-end edition 1999

their social circumstances. Paul Farmer's book, *Women, Poverty, and AIDS: Sex, Drugs, and Structural Violence,* brilliantly draws the connection between poverty, sex, money, and drug use. Farmer argues that drug users usually "hang with" other drug users and that females will spend time with male "drug partners" because of their perceived notion that they will be "protected." This protection comes with a high price, however, because these women increase their risk of HIV through sharing of needles and having sex with men who may be infected with HIV. The stories of Debi, Sally, and Regina demonstrate that it is not only protection that they sought as drug users, but also familiarity. These people and their lifestyles were all they knew, so they "hung" with their own kind, which led to persistent high-risk behavior.

Drug use and poverty are also tied to social behaviors that govern sex and money. It is fair to say that many drug users are in deep despair and struggling to survive. In this equation, a woman who is exchanging sex for drugs or sex for money has little power to negotiate condom use, hence placing herself in severe danger for HIV infection. The drug-use lifestyle also places women at further risk through exposure to assault and rape. Studies have indicated that commercial female sex workers are in great danger from sexual violence by their male clients and intimate partners, whether they are drug users or not.[86]

Intravenous drug use among Native people is becoming more and more prevalent in urban, rural, and reservation communities. In South Dakota, for example, "at least a third of the AIDS cases in Native Americans are a result of injection drug use or having a partner that injects drugs."[87] Activist Carole LaFavor (Ojibway) believes that there is a lack of attention to Native American drug users due to the mistaken belief that Natives do not use drugs other than alcohol. This misunderstanding was further supported as recently as 1989 when researchers reported that there was a "low intravenous drug usage among Indians."[88]

LaFavor confronts the myth that Native people are not drug users in a video in which she discusses how she contracted HIV through intravenous drug use and how she used drugs with other Native people.[89] LaFavor's declaration that drug use is a problem is supported by John Bird, a consultant from Bozeman, Montana, who publicly stated that "intravenous drug use is epidemic on some reservations."[90]

Women have taken an active role in HIV/AIDS prevention. In hopes of protecting Native Americans and fulfilling her vision, LaFavor has become an AIDS activist. She is the editor of a newsletter for HIV-positive Natives, *Positively Native,* and has participated in many Native American AIDS videos, including *American Indians Against HIV/AIDS Leadership Project: Presentation by Carole LaFavor; An Interruption in the Journey;* and *Her Giveaway: A Spiritual Journey with AIDS.* LaFavor is also a national AIDS activist who advocates the use of alternative medicine in conjunction with western medicine. She speaks at legislative hearings and works for increased access to quality health care for Native people. LaFavor is following her vision, which is to talk to people about AIDS and to help prevent one more person from becoming infected.

With few resources, two other Native HIV/AIDS-infected women, Barbara Byron and Lisa Tiger, join LaFavor in spreading the word about AIDS through videos. Byron's video *I'm Not Afraid of Me* is her personal story of being a young Native Alaskan woman who contracted the HIV virus through heterosexual contact, and then passed the infection to her daughter. Lisa Tiger's (Muscogee Creek/Cherokee) video, *Lisa Tiger's Story,* discusses how she contracted HIV heterosexually at the age of twenty-seven, and how she feels that it is her duty to educate Native people about AIDS. In the video Tiger is shown in an open discussion with Native students from Haskell's Indian Junior College.

LaFavor, Byron, and Tiger have been driven to tell their personal stories because of their love and concern for their communities. Joining them in their fight against HIV/AIDS are noninfected women who also have a desire to warn tribal people and communities. Native American female producers and/or directors have used their talents to fight the spread of AIDS by creating culturally specific Native American videos. Sandra Osawa's (Makah) *AIDS and the Native American Family,* one of the first Native AIDS videos produced, presents the story of an urban Native man who gives AIDS to his pregnant Native wife before he dies. This story advocates strong family and community ties as a source of prevention and the use of spirituality for healing. Another woman, Mona Smith (Lakota), has worked independently on AIDS videos and in conjunction with Native organizations. Smith's videos, *Her Giveaway: A Spiritual Journey with AIDS* and *An Interruption in the Journey,* are funded, in part, by the Native American Minnesota AIDS Project.

Women are also working in other ways to address HIV/AIDS. Sharon Day (Ojibway), executive director of the Minnesota American Indian AIDS Task Force, serves a large group of urban Natives in the Minneapolis area. Under her directorship the Task Force provides case management, outreach, technical assistance, peer education, a two-spirit risk reduction program, and a monthly newsletter focusing on current AIDS-related issues. The Task Force also serves as a clearinghouse for educational materials from around the country.

Task Force programs are culturally specific, and some are geared specifically to Native women. The needs of Native women include Native support groups and spiritual healing. The Task Force's Talking Circle for American Indian women is a good example of how to address gender and culturally specific needs. It includes traditional forms of counseling (Talking Circles), and provides transportation, childcare, and meals to participants. In the Talking Circles, the women smudge, pray, and at times do Indian crafts as they discuss the impacts of HIV on their lives and families.[91] Childcare is critical since most Native women must bring their children with them. The American Indian Community House HIV/AIDS project has recently added female Talking Circles as well as a project called Visiting Aunties, which provides home visits to help HIV/AIDS-infected tribal members.[92]

The type of work that the Minnesota American Indian AIDS Task Force and American Indian Community House are involved in is carried out in a reservation setting by another organization comprised of women dedicated to Native women's health issues – the Native American Women's Health Education Resource Center (Women's Center). Both the Task Force and the Women's Center are prime examples of self-determination for medical self-sufficiency among family and community members and are positive models for other communities. It is clear that women must, and are, taking control

over their own medical treatment, prevention, disease intervention, and recovery; it is under these circumstances that they become models for what
others can do.

Opened in 1988, the Women's Center was the first organization on a
reservation to address the needs of Native women and also the first in South
Dakota to provide AIDS education. Director Charon Asetoyer was honored
in 1998 for ten years of dedicated leadership of this organization. The entire budget of the Women's Center is approximately $450,000 and they have
fourteen full and part-time staff members. Programs include community
organizing and leadership development, domestic violence prevention,
child development, adult learning, cancer prevention, reproductive health,
and scholarships for Native women. Concerned about the rise of domestic
violence in Indian country, the center is currently studying the reasons behind the increase. Their curriculum is holistic, incorporating HIV/AIDS prevention and treatment as an integral component of their programs. The center decided years ago not just to focus on HIV prevention, but "to focus on
incorporating HIV intervention, prevention, education and services across
the board into all their programming."[93] The organization incorporates
HIV/AIDS prevention and treatment into its women's shelter work, youth
groups, adult learning, and other programs.

Since there are so many factors placing Native women at risk, an effective curriculum must not only address the health and medical aspects of
HIV but critical factors such as poverty and powerlessness as well. These are
addressed by the Women's Center in their programs in adult learning, domestic violence, and community and organization leadership. The Women's
Center thus works against the social forces that undermine women's ca-
pacity to adopt and sustain healthy lifestyles.

The development of self-esteem and personal power is especially critical in combating the spread of HIV/AIDS because of the stigma attached to
the disease. For women, the stigma is layered on top of the perception of
HIV/AIDS as a disease of immorality and deviance: a gay disease and a drug
user disease, it has become a disease that "bad women" contract. For Native
women, this societal perspective of inferiority and immorality is not new,
however. Historically, they have been represented in literature and art according to the "virgin-whore" dichotomy. Hence, empowerment and the
building of self-esteem are of particular importance to Native women.

The Women's Center also addresses the affects of the disease on community, parents, siblings, sexual partners, and children. It holds workshops for
many groups, including high school students, spiritual leaders, and families. Various programs instruct trainers, provide counseling before and after

HIV tests, and assist with problem solving for people with AIDS and their families. The family support is essential because women with HIV/AIDS are greatly concerned about their children and their needs. Pregnant women with HIV/AIDS worry not only about passing the disease to their babies, but about the psychological well being of their kids, and the discrimination they may face. Many Native women have stressed that at diagnosis they were less concerned about themselves and more concerned about their children and how their disease would impact them. They also stressed how important it is to make sure that somebody will be there to take care of their children when they are no longer around.

Good education is one of the keys to successful support for those with HIV/AIDS. The Women's Center sponsors a peer counselor program that trains high school students to talk about AIDS with their fellow students. Knowing the importance of how AIDS information is disseminated in a Native setting, the dedicated staff at the Women's Center wisely calls upon and trains Native spiritual leaders, women, and Native youth. In addition to addressing women-specific issues, the Women's Center for a time extended their AIDS work to include Sun Dance participants.[94] The Sun Dance is primarily a ritual of self-sacrifice. An individual, making a vow to the Great Spirit, will pledge to fast, pray, and dance for several days for the well being of the people. This very sacred and profound ceremony is conducted by many Plains Indians and has been practiced since time immemorial. It is mainly conducted to provide health, prosperity, and healing for Native communities. For the Lakota people, the Sun Dance is one of the seven sacred rites given to them by White Buffalo Calf Woman and taught to a holy man in a vision. Some Sun Dance ceremonies include the piercing of the chest or back and skin offerings as a sacrifice to the Great Spirit for the well being of the people. These activities have the potential of spreading infection. The Women's Center worked with the spiritual leaders, those who were pierced, and those who made skin offerings to educate them about AIDS, recommend specific Sun Dance precautions, and distribute more than ten thousand scalpels to the dancers and other participants. The budget of twenty-five thousand dollars for this special project came from the Indian Health Service. However, it barely paid for staff, phones, and travel and, as of summer 1998, was cut entirely and the money placed in the hands of the Indian Health Service.[95]

The Women's Center teaches tribal adults and children through the use of videos and has developed several AIDS videos.[96] The video *It Can Happen to Anybody* presents the story of two AIDS-infected Natives, one male and one female, who talk about the reactions of their families and communities to their diagnosis. They discuss how they were discriminated against by their community, church, and other tribal members. Their situation reinforces the tribal health officials' concerns that Native people are not exempt from HIV/AIDS. The center's other video, *Mom and Sons Series,* is a cartoon with three sections directed toward different age groups. The sections can be viewed together or individually. Section 1, "What is AIDS?" is presented in simple language and is aimed at children from kindergarten to fifth grade. This section shows a young Indian child, Sam, asking his mother about AIDS because his friend John has AIDS. His mother responds by telling Sam what AIDS stands for and some of the ways it is not transmitted, such as "by sharing a Popsicle." Section 2, "Is John Going to Die?" (aimed at grades four through seven) continues the story of Sam and John, but the children are older and the language more complex. In this section, Sam not only asks his mother more questions about AIDS, but he also visits John in the hospital where he speaks to John and his doctor about having AIDS. This section contains more details about AIDS and its physical consequences. Made for an older audience (grades six through twelve), section 3, "How Do People Get AIDS?" portrays John and his mother holding a more in-depth conversation about the causes of AIDS and how people can protect themselves. Native music and cultural and visual texture are prominent throughout both of the videos.

There are many more Native women working to empower, heal, and protect themselves and their communities. These women and the ones I have named should be honored. Faced with the alarming and daunting task of saving their own lives and the lives of their communities, these women are approaching AIDS education, prevention, and care with dedication, hard work, creativity, and love. By examining their work, scholars, researchers, health officials, AIDS activists, and Native AIDS organizations will gain valuable insights into the ways Native women are positively influencing their own health and their communities. The acts of these women, on behalf of those affected by HIV/AIDS, ensure that Native women will neither be silenced nor invisible in the epidemic; concurrently, their work is overturning the dangerous belief that AIDS is only a man's disease.

Through their dedication and storytelling, Native women are able to articulate their long-standing concerns and to influence the development of AIDS/HIV resources, identify and address a variety of women's health concerns, and work on community building and empowerment to ensure the survival of women, men, and children.

# NATIVE AMERICAN YOUTH
## AND HIV/AIDS

*Our Future*

1 2 **3** 4

Life for youth today is extremely difficult. They live in a world with increasing violence and poverty, and rising HIV infection. This chapter begins with the story of Mike, who was born into poverty and contracted HIV in his teens. Mike's story illuminates the life of youth who are not only born into poverty but also raised in homes without structure, stability, and nurturing. His story demonstrates how some youth, whose basic needs are not met during childhood, are driven to fulfill their needs of security and love in unhealthy and risky ways.

### MIKE

Mike was born on a reservation in Arizona in 1970 to a Native mother and non-Native father. His mother had met his father in school and married him at an early age. He has two brothers and one sister. He considered his "growing up years not too good." His father was a drinker, abusive, and sold drugs. His early childhood memories include "family get-togethers where there was drinking and someone always getting beat up."

Eventually his mother took the kids and left his father. During this separation, when Mike was around eight years old, he remembers a police officer coming to the house to tell his mother that his father had committed suicide in jail. From that point on his mother began moving around a lot. Although his mother had separated from his father because he was physically abusive and an excessive drinker, she too drank excessively. Mike remembers her going on binges and leaving for days. Mike and his older brother were responsible for taking care of their little sister. At that time Mike was ten years old and given a tremendous amount of responsibility. When his mother was gone he would always "wonder if she was going to come back home." Mike said that she had a scare one time when she had his baby sister in the car and she blacked out from drinking. She received a ticket that night for drinking and driving. At that point she attempted to get her life together, but she was unable to stay sober.

Mike remembers being a very "angry child" and he took his first drink at age eleven. As he got older he began to "disrespect my mother for some of the things she did when I was a child and from the abuse I had gotten from her." He was also angry because he did not have a male figure to look up to or have as support. His mother had male friends but Mike said, "they really did not contribute much and they were alcoholics." Mike saw his home as being an "unhappy place" and as he started to get older "little by little I became a problem."

When Mike was fourteen his mother moved the family off the reservation to San Francisco. This was the first time Mike had ever been in a big city and he began to explore his sexuality. He had his first sexual experience with another male in San Francisco when he was fourteen. He was unsure about his homosexual identity but in the city he became more and more accepting of who he was and realized that there was nothing wrong with it.

His home was still unstable in the city and he began to meet other troubled kids – kids on the street who were runaways. The kids he met told him that he was attractive and that he could make good money through prostitution. Shortly thereafter he began prostituting himself and experimenting with drugs.

The men he was servicing were usually older and he liked what he was doing because he felt that they "treated me like an adult." Mike wanted to be treated like an adult because he was not treated that way at home. He began to exchange sex for drugs, money, and "just because people desired me." He talked about how he "wanted to be and feel loved." He became difficult to manage for his single-parent mother; he rarely went to school and ran away a lot.

Mike left home when he was eighteen years old. At that time he "hooked up in a relationship with an old friend." This was Mike's first "real" relationship and he felt like he loved him, although he knew his partner was cheating on him. Mike's partner, Mark, was thirty years old and he took good care of Mike. He even took him to Europe. On their way home from Europe Mark became ill. Mike watched as his health began to deteriorate. He became so ill that Mike had the responsibility of taking care of him. Mike began to remember how he had to take care of his younger sister when he was young, and he began to resent the role. At the young age of eighteen Mike felt trapped at home, but he continued to care for Mark even though he felt, many times, that Mark did not really love him. Eventually Mark had to be hospitalized. He told Mike not to visit him because he was too sick, but he asked Mike to call him on the phone regularly.

Within two years Mark died. Before he died, however, he told Mike to come visit. When Mike went to the hospital Mark's family was there and they told him "Mark has AIDS and he is going to die." Mike had not known Mark had AIDS, nor that he had been diagnosed with the disease several years before. With the urging of Mark's family Mike took an AIDS test. It came back positive. He was nineteen years old at the time.

Mike did not respond well to his diagnosis. He lived with another Native man and they both began to drink excessively. At times he was even homeless. He said, "I knew I had the virus and was afraid, but my alcoholism started to take off." He fell into an abyss and slowly began to destroy himself. He said he was basically "waiting to die." Horrible things began to happen to him and he was continually in trouble. Then one day, he realized that he did not want to die. He realized that if AIDS did not kill him he was either going to overdose or die from alcohol poisoning and he knew he needed help. He came to realize that he did not want to live life on the streets anymore because it was "too hard." He even became suicidal, but at the end he chose recovery instead. This was three and a half years after his HIV diagnosis. When he began his recovery program he realized that he could not even remember the last time he had been sober.

Today, Mike is sober and has been living with the HIV infection for over ten years. He has reestablished his relationship with his family, who help support him through his illnesses. Mike uses a number of urban Native agencies to deal with treatment and care. He also attends Native sweats and meets with traditional healers.

He also has gained a sense of responsibility and wants to give back to the Native and San Francisco communities. He feels that it is important to reach out to troubled youth because he can relate to them. He believes that the street youth of today are "harder than what they used to be when I was there" and that they need direction. Mike is actively involved in youth outreach and he goes to schools to "talk about my experiences of having HIV and to help kids make important choices in their lives." He says, "I don't want them to do what I have done!" Mike concluded his interview with words for kids on the street, "don't give up, and try to live a healthy life. Be healthy as possible. Don't give up."

The future of all societies depends on the children; hence the fundamental importance of their health and well being. Along with other serious challenges, today's youth face the challenge of maintaining their health. World-

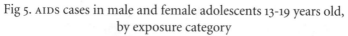

Fig 5. AIDS cases in male and female adolescents 13-19 years old,
by exposure category

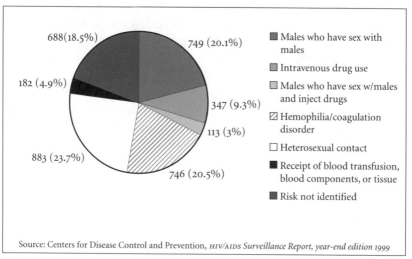

688(18.5%)  749 (20.1%)
182 (4.9%)
347 (9.3%)
113 (3%)
883 (23.7%)
746 (20.5%)

■ Males who have sex with males

■ Intravenous drug use

□ Males who have sex w/males and inject drugs

▨ Hemophilia/coagulation disorder

□ Heterosexual contact

■ Receipt of blood transfusion, blood components, or tissue

■ Risk not identified

Source: Centers for Disease Control and Prevention, *HIV/AIDS Surveillance Report, year-end edition 1999*

wide, one out of every two people with HIV becomes infected between the ages of fifteen and twenty-four.[1] With five young people becoming infected every minute, the HIV/AIDS pandemic poses a serious health threat to the children of the world. Every day, sixteen hundred people under the age of fifteen are infected with HIV.

In the developing world HIV infection in children is acquired mainly through breast-feeding; in 1997, 590,000 kids were infected by their mothers.[2] In the United States AIDS-related illnesses are the sixth leading cause of death among young people fifteen to twenty-four years old.[3] In addition, one-fourth of all new HIV infections in the United States are estimated to be among those under twenty-one, and most people who developed AIDS before thirty were infected with HIV in their teen years.[4] As of December 1999 the total number of AIDS cases for youth thirteen to twenty-four was 29,629 and of HIV infection 21,246.[5] In adolescents between the ages of thirteen and nineteen there were 3,725 AIDS cases, and the main route of transmission was heterosexual contact (fig. 5). The rise of HIV among the young is of great concern to Native people because a high percentage of their population is young. Approximately half of the Native American population is under 27.2 years of age. This is quite different from the white population, whose median age is 37.4 years.[6]

Although AIDS cases have decreased overall, HIV infection rates have continued to rise. Concern over the increase in HIV cases has prompted the CDC to target prevention efforts toward youth, particularly African Americans and Latinos.[7] African American youth have been targeted because they represented 63 percent of all new adolescent and young adult HIV infections from January 1994 to June 1997.[8] An examination of HIV prevalence rates among youth in the Job Corps revealed that rates were higher in women than in men in the same age group.[9] In addition, young females between ages thirteen and twenty-four made up 49 percent of the HIV cases in that age group as of December 1999.[10] Among Native Americans HIV infection, as of June 1999, is the "eighth leading cause of mortality for those between 15 and 34 years living on or near reservations."[11]

The main risk factors for HIV infection in our youth are sexual intercourse, alcohol, and substance abuse (including intravenous drug use). Thus it is critical that AIDS organizations, tribes, health officials, and activists remain honest with adolescents about these issues. The need for awareness and honesty was emphasized by Ron Rowell at a recent AIDS conference focused on school-age children and adolescents. Rowell stated that we must admit to one another openly that many of our kids are having sex, and that we have high rates of STDs and teen pregnancy in our communities. He also asked that "we not bury our heads regarding sexual behaviors of some adolescent Indian males who have sex with other males." He further noted how Native kids become part of the drug culture and move on quickly to injecting drugs. Others are, or have been, sexually abused. Some end up on the streets trading their bodies for money, food, or drugs because their families have fallen apart, or because their parents discovered they were gay and booted them out of the house and out of their lives. These conditions, Rowell argues, must be admitted before changes can take place.[12]

Facing reality is the beginning of change, and a starting point is the acknowledgment that sex is the main route of transmission for our youth. The ability to communicate with our youth is also important, and in some areas of Indian country we are not doing that. For example, in developing HIV/AIDS curricula for Native American youth in the Southwest, the Native American Prevention Project Against AIDS and Substance Abuse found that "across gender and between adolescents and adults . . . topics dealing with sexual activity, pregnancy, contraception and sexually transmitted diseases were reported as rare."[13] Communication is vital in stopping the spread of HIV/AIDS among adolescents, and it would benefit us to begin an open discussion about sex and sexual development with our children.

Adolescence is a time when young boys and girls are experiencing sexual feelings and finding their sexuality. The CDC reports that seven out of ten high school twelfth graders have had sexual intercourse, 23 percent have had four or more partners, and less than half of sexually active twelfth graders report using latex condoms consistently.[14] Other studies estimate that "57 percent of U.S. teenagers have engaged in intercourse by age 17, and most with more than one partner."[15] And over half of all young women have had sexual intercourse by age eighteen.[16] A study of Native women in Montana, ages fifteen to twenty-four, concluded that "10 percent of on-reservation and 13.6 percent of off-reservation women reported age at first sexual intercourse of 14 years or younger." The same finding has been supported in a national study with a larger sampling.[17] In Alaska 59 percent of Alaskan Native mothers have their first child under the age of twenty, as compared to 24 percent among other races in the United States.[18]

With early sexual activity come sexually transmitted diseases. STDs are the "second most commonly diagnosed infectious disease in adolescents . . . with sixty-six percent of all STDs occurring in persons under age 25."[19] The CDC believes that STD treatment will reduce the spread of HIV; this is an important approach, since it is estimated that three million of the twelve million new cases a year in the United States occur among teenagers thirteen to nineteen years old.[20]

The large number of youth who are sexually active is frightening to think about because many are not developmentally prepared. It has been found that adolescents between the ages of twelve and fourteen think in the present, have "difficulty projecting themselves into the future . . . are less able to see the implication of their actions on their futures and are less able to take responsibility."[21] Mike, for example, began to engage in prostitution at age fourteen and did not consider the consequences of his actions or think about using condoms. This kind of thinking, which is a natural part of growing up, can be extremely dangerous in the light of HIV transmission. Thus, knowing how our youth think and act is critical in implementing HIV/AIDS programs and education. For example, a study assessing the degree of concern that Native American adolescents from reservation communities had about contracting HIV/AIDS found that 55 percent were not concerned.[22] A 1994 study of Lakota youth noted that they were worried about contracting AIDS, but the study did not explore whether that concern translated into safe behavior.[23] Another study of Native teenagers found that "among all students surveyed, regardless of gender or sexual activity, [only] 40 percent were concerned about contracting AIDS." Compared to their non-Native peers, Native teens were "half as likely" to use contraceptives.[24] The lack of concern about contracting HIV/AIDS, combined with intercourse at younger ages and inconsistent condom use means we have a "bomb" ready to explode.

An encouraging sign, however, is a survey of fourteen thousand Native adolescents that found that 60 percent of sexually active youth "were quite concerned about getting AIDS or an STD." Yet this healthy fear did not always translate into action. A high proportion of sexually active youth used no contraception at all – 29 percent of males and 44 percent of females.[25] Apparently, STD knowledge and continual education are critical in stopping the spread of HIV/AIDS. The need for continual education can be seen through an examination of youth from the Yankton Sioux Reservation. A study of Yankton youth ages fourteen to nineteen found that "the 18 and 19 year old women were a lot more aware of reproductive tract infections than youth ages 14–15." It was noted, however, that the older group received education and information in school when they were fourteen and fifteen years old. The newer group of fourteen and fifteen year olds, however, did not receive information because the governor of South Dakota signed a bill in 1995 stating that HIV education no longer needed to be taught in schools within the state.[26]

Continued HIV education as well as accurate knowledge will help change some attitudes that place adolescents at risk. For example, while older male gay men see AIDS as a disease of the youth, adolescents today believe that AIDS is a disease of older gay men. Studies of gay adolescent males suggest that this idea is a result of "the prolonged latency period of HIV infection." Adolescent males "feel unthreatened by a disease that they think will not affect them for 10 years." [27] A study of ten to nineteen year olds in the rural Southwest found that Native American youth knew more about AIDS than African American youth and less than Caucasian youth; yet they held a fair number of misperceptions that could lead to the adoption or continuance of unsafe sexual practices.[28] The study concluded that outreach was critical in rural areas because these youth would eventually migrate to urban areas – where the prevalence of HIV/AIDS is higher – for work, school, and medical services.

Knowledge about HIV/AIDS is irrelevant, however, unless one acts on it. Surveys of students at tribal colleges revealed that while students were aware of HIV/AIDS and felt that AIDS education should be provided in public schools, they were only "moderately concerned that AIDS will affect their lives." [29] Another attitude that places our youth in danger is that risk is "a badge of maturity." [30]

Slowing the spread of HIV infection among our youth requires not only close attention to adolescent beliefs and attitudes but a better understanding of the difference between sexual behavior and sexual orientation. A common misconception, for example, is that if a person is homosexual, then he or she engages exclusively in same-sex relations. A study of the psychosexual development of lesbian and gay adolescents demonstrated that heterosexuality was a common activity.[31] Little research has been done on adolescent sexual behavior, however, and it is critical that we work toward broadening our understanding. Research on youth and issues of HIV/AIDS is also important because adolescents, in general, have been ignored in the epidemic. And, although some adolescents have participated in clinical trials and service delivery, overall their specific needs are not addressed.[32]

Some research indicates that youth are aware of HIV/AIDS and how it is transmitted but continue to engage in high-risk behavior. A recent study of runaway, homeless, and incarcerated youth reported that most had some knowledge about HIV/AIDS but their knowledge was incomplete – placing them at further risk.[33] Mike, who lived and "hung out" with homeless and runaway youth, said he didn't know anything about HIV/AIDS and that lots of people were having unprotected sex.

Although adolescents as a group are vulnerable to HIV infection, certain subgroups are at even higher risk. In 1993 the National Commission on HIV/AIDS recommended that "national prevention initiatives address the prevention of HIV infection in adolescents, particularly youth in high-risk situations."[34] Adolescent subgroups at high risk include runaways and homeless youth, those involved in the juvenile system, those who attend alternative schools, gay/bisexuals, victims of assault (including rape and sexual assault), and minorities. Every year an estimated 1 to 1.3 million teens run away from home and many of them will exchange sex for shelter, security, food, and drugs. Mike was clearly a youth at risk of infection once he began to run away and started to exchange sex for drugs, money, and love.

Incarcerated youth are another high-risk group. They have been found to "lack future orientation, have poor self-image, and perceive little or no value in modifying risk behaviors."[35] A study of detained youth in rural Alabama reported that they engaged in high-risk sexual activities such as unprotected sex with multiple partners and the commodification of sex.[36] In general both runaways and detained/incarcerated youth take unnecessary and potentially dangerous risks.

Students at alternative high schools (over 280,000 students nationwide) are another high-risk group. A recent survey of risk behavior found that 87.8 percent of alternative high school students had sexual intercourse and 45.9 percent of that group had sex within the three months preceding the survey;

a little less than half used condoms. More alarming is that 22 percent had sexual intercourse before age thirteen and half had about four sexual partners.[37] Alternative high school students also have other high-risk factors in their lives, such as high rates of drug use and violence.

High-school dropouts are another high-risk subgroup because of high rates of drug use and violence. A 1996 study that examined drug use, violence, and victimization among various ethnic dropouts, including Native youth, found that dropouts had higher rates of drug involvement and were "more likely both to perpetrate and be victims of violence."[38]

Young gay/bisexual men are a subgroup at the highest risk of HIV infection. Although unprotected sex is the main route of transmission, homophobic attitudes that they confront contribute to their high-risk behaviors. A study of attitudes in rural areas toward people with AIDS demonstrated that Native American and African American youth had the lowest tolerance for people with AIDS, with many believing that "people who died from AIDS deserved what they got, that they should be barred from school, and [respondents] would be upset to find themselves alone with a gay person."[39] The most distressing aspect of this attitude is that there is a higher prevalence of homosexual and bisexual identification and behavior among adolescent Natives than among Anglo-American adolescents, according to a recent study of sexual orientation.[40] The researchers in this study, however, call into question the "cultural relevancy" of its methodology because there was a large number of unsure responses. In addressing the uncertainty of their findings, the researchers called for the creation of more culturally sensitive research methods, as well as recommending that those working with Native youth be more diligent in assessing their sexual behavior and making sure that prevention materials be all-inclusive, including hetero-, homo-, and bisexual activities.

Sending positive messages to young gay/bisexual youth is critical to their well being and health. Many of these adolescents feel that they have no support and turn to alcohol and drugs. Compared to heterosexual youth, gay, lesbian, bisexual, and transgender (GLBT) youth are "twice as likely to use alcohol, three times more likely to use marijuana and to show signs of serious substance abuse, and eight times more likely to use cocaine" – all of which place them at great risk for HIV infection.[41] In addition, 80 percent of GLBT youth have a sense of isolation, both socially and emotionally.

Living with a stigma has forced many gay/bisexual youth into high-risk behavior. For example, when Darrell Joe, a young Navajo man, "came out," he starting drinking at gay bars where he was able to experiment with his "gay side."[42] Many have been forced to leave home because of their sexual orientation, pushing some into prostitution.[43] These youth also experience a high incidence of violence and high school drop-out rates.[44]

It has been argued that young men who have sex with men may misperceive their risk of HIV transmission. In a presentation in Los Angeles it was noted that sixty-four percent of young Native American gay/bisexual men reported unprotected anal intercourse.[45] This was higher than for any other ethnic group.

Many gay/bisexual youth begin to believe they are destined to die of AIDS, hence they do not engage in long-term relationships, they suffer from low self-esteem and depression, they engage in reckless behavior, and they attempt suicide. Sadly, suicide is too common among our youth in general – in 1998, 8 percent of students in grades nine through twelve had attempted suicide, and suicide among children between ages ten and fourteen has doubled in the past two decades.[46] The general sense of loneliness and depression is exacerbated in young men who have sex with men. These youth are seven times more likely to attempt suicide than heterosexual youth.[47] One study found that among gay/bisexual youth of color, 41 percent of females and 35 percent of males had attempted suicide.[48]

In general, Native youth live stressful lives and many are suffering from depression, which may lead to substance abuse and suicide.[49] Native American annual suicide rates are 44 per 100,000 for fifteen- to twenty-four- year-olds, but this does not capture variability among the different tribes. For example, the rate among Chippewas is 6 per 100,000 while the Blackfeet rate is 130 per 100,000.[50] The Navajos were shown to have low suicide rates overall, but researcher Carol Sullivan noted in another study that suicide among Native Americans is particularly high among young men, hence she feared that HIV-infected Navajos are at a great risk for suicide.[51] Darrell Joe, the young Navajo mentioned earlier, attempted suicide twice after his diagnosis of HIV, as did Mike.[52] Darrell and Mike, however, are not alone in their response to a positive diagnosis. Suicide is high among AIDS patients in general. In New York, for instance, the suicide rate is 681 per 100,000 for men who have AIDS, which is thirty-six times the rate of New York men who do not have the disease.[53]

Alcohol and drug use among gay/bisexual adolescents is also high. Use of alcohol and drugs is found not only among the gay/bisexual risk group but also among rural kids and high school youth in general. Contrary to many studies that suggest drug use is more prevalent in urban areas, a recent study found that "adolescents in small-town and rural America are much more likely than their peers in urban centers to have used drugs."[54] It has been reported that 89 percent of high school seniors have tried alcohol and four out of ten have tried marijuana.[55] In addition, a recent CDC report notes that one of every fifty high school students has injected an illegal drug.[56]

Fred Beauvais, a psychologist who has been studying alcohol and drug use among Native American youth for over twenty years, notes that drug use patterns of Native youth follow trends for youth nationwide, although their rates are higher. Drug use increased in the early 1980s and then declined through 1992. Based on reservation reports and survey data, Beauvais suggests that drug use is on an increase again.[57] This possibility is frightening since drug and alcohol use poses the same problems for adolescents as for adults; impaired judgment and lower inhibitions, which may lead to risky sexual behavior. As noted by Beauvais, "for over 25 years it's been recognized that substance use and abuse has been a significant problem for large numbers of Indian youth residing on reservations."[58] In dealing with the rise of HIV in adolescents, it would thus be wise for health officials to take substance use into account as they create prevention/intervention adolescent materials.

Native communities have not let their guard down and are facing this challenge head on. For example, during the summer of 1999, Native community members and four schools in the Wagner, South Dakota, area participated in a Walk/Run event to draw attention to drug use, particularly methamphetamine use. The event was organized in response to some very alarming facts: South Dakota's per capita use of methamphetamines was similar to use in large cities such as Miami and Houston; the Office of National Drug Control Policy designated South Dakota as a High Intensity Drug Traffic Area; and 13 percent of high school students in South Dakota reported using methamphetamines.[59] Charon Asetoyer maintains that methamphetamine use is "ravaging communities on the reservation" and that because of the high number of diabetics there is "no lack of syringes." Her concerns over drug use and syringes extend to the community's volatility with regard to HIV and hepatitis risks.[60]

Alcohol use among Native adolescents has been studied for many years. Early studies demonstrated that more Native youth consumed alcohol than non-Natives: out of a sample of fourteen hundred Native youth in grades seven to twelve, 82 percent had used alcohol, compared to 66 percent of non-Natives.[61] Beauvais, one of the most prolific writers on this topic, stresses how difficult it is for Native youth in an Indian community to deal with alcoholism because "they grow up in a world where there are multiple, conflicting conceptualizations about the nature of alcohol and its effects on people."[62] He argues that Native youth get a multitude of contradictory messages about alcohol use, which makes it difficult to make healthy choices. Beauvais calls for a critical approach to alcohol prevention among Native youth because it will assist young people in sorting out their own perceptions and values regarding alcohol. He believes that by working closely with youth we may find that adult perceptions and adolescent perceptions are miles apart.[63]

Beauvais is not alone in his advice to listen to Native youth. Theresa O'Nell and Christian Mitchell have found that the contemporary lack of attention to the cultural context of Native teen drinking has weakened the field. They suggest that we question youth because it is important to document the drinking environment and analyze the role of normative drinking within the larger sociocultural system, paying close attention to the values that guide those drinking judgments.[64] Listening to our youth is critical in the work against alcohol use among youth as well as in HIV/AIDS prevention.

Reasons for drinking and drug use among young people vary. Among Alaskan Native youth, for example, a sense of complete hopelessness has been found to be a factor in teen drinking and drug use. The hopelessness found among Alaskan Native youth stems in part from the process of acculturation. Many of the village youth endure a move from a traditional and nurturing environment to school and/or work and are thus confronted with an alien and unsupportive urban environment.[65]

Alcohol and drug abuse are also frequently tied to childhood trauma. Many of America's youth are victims of assault; nationwide, approximately half of rape victims are adolescents.[66] Although the majority of these victims are young women, males are also victims.

Childhood trauma results in a variety of psychological and behavioral consequences that can increase risk of HIV infection. A study in the early 1990s found that survivors of childhood sexual abuse were four times more likely than non-abused participants to report having worked as a prostitute and were more likely to engage in sexual activities with casual acquaintances. Studies have also demonstrated that adults and youth who have experienced childhood trauma have been associated with a variety of high-risk behaviors such as a greater number of sexual partners, more unprotected sex involving drugs, early use of intravenous drugs, an inability to negotiate condom use, and engagement in unwanted sexual activity, as well as more sexually transmitted diseases.[67] This cycle of unhealthy behavior was shown in Mike's story. He was born into poverty, endured early childhood trauma and abuse, and then engaged in high-risk behaviors in his teens. It is evident that this segment of America's youth are in grave danger of HIV infection.

Native youth are part of this segment of society. In 1992 the Foundations of Indian Teens project conducted a survey focusing on teens and trauma. The study found that 51 percent had experienced a traumatic event and 37 percent said they had experienced more than one.[68] Similarly, the Health Survey of Indian Boarding Schools (grades nine to twelve) found that 60 percent of young tribal members had experienced or witnessed at least one traumatic event. Both studies also found that these young people displayed symptoms of posttraumatic stress disorder.[69] Another study, which surveyed 13,454 Native American and Alaskan youth in grades seven through twelve, found that 18 percent had experienced some form of abuse and "overall ten percent reported sexual abuse while thirteen percent indicated that they had been physically abused."[70] The same study revealed that abuse increased with age, and "by the 12th grade, 23.9% of females reported having been physically abused, and 21.6% reported sexual abuse." Alaskan youth are known to experience extremely high rates of sexual assault – with "53 percent of the Alaskan children [the majority are Native Alaskan youth] in state custody for abuse or neglect."[71]

As discussed in chapter 2, economics plays a large role in the spread of HIV/AIDS among adults, and the issues raised there are applicable to youth, too. Many youth, particularly youth of color, in America are born into poverty. In Alaska, for example, youth aged five to seventeen are three times more likely to live in poverty than Alaskans of all races.[72] This places them at risk because their health and well being are likely to be neglected.

Economics also plays a significant role in the spread of HIV/AIDS among young women of color. As noted in the previous chapter, STD rates among Native people are very high, and the same is true for all young women of color. The lack of income, health insurance, and access to health care or health information, particularly about HIV/AIDS, places these young women at great risk for infection because they will not know how to protect themselves.[73] Lack of income may also prevent them from treating their STDs, which can be conduits for HIV infection.

Another social factor that places both young women and men in danger is having sex with older partners. Studies show that "a quarter of sexually active men ages 22–26 years and nineteen percent of males ages 20–21 years report sexual intercourse with a teenage partner during the last year and many Latina and African American adolescent females have reported first sexual intercourse with older male partners."[74] Older men have a higher chance of having HIV because they may have injected drugs, had more sexual partners, and had a variety of sexual experiences. The socialization of young women will also determine the degree of protection from

HIV. In general young women tend not to be assertive, making it extremely difficult for them to be assertive about safe sex, particularly if their partners are older.[75]

Young gay men who have sex with older men also have problems negotiating condoms, and are placed in a high-risk position if the older man has had many sexual experiences. Darrell Joe, the young Navajo man who contracted HIV from his sexual partner, thought his partner was twenty-three or twenty-four years old but instead was "32 and had just gotten out of prison."[76] Mike also engaged in a relationship with an older man who passed the HIV infection on to him. A study conducted in San Francisco in 1994 noted that although young men who have sex with men are aware of HIV/AIDS and how it is transmitted, they still had unprotected sex for reasons that include the belief that AIDS is an older man's disease, being in love, substance use, and an inability to negotiate condoms.[77]

Native youth have suggested that prevention materials need to be directed to different populations because issues are different for urban and reservation youth. They also believe that Native urban youth are more aware of sexual topics, including HIV/AIDS, and that it is more critical to assess the needs of reservation youth.[78] Prevention among this group must address their complex and diverse needs.

One critical need for adolescents is to negotiate condom use. In an effort to give youth the skills needed to stay safe and empower them to make good choices, many agencies have created a role for interactive teaching methodologies that include self-esteem building and peer educators. In California, where AIDS rates are high for the general population as well as for Native populations, several Native health organizations have created prevention programs that are geared toward self-esteem building and self-empowerment. The San Diego American Indian Health Center and the Native American Health Center in Oakland have created programs emphasizing community and cultural pride because they realize that adolescents will not be responsive to messages about prevention and behavioral changes until they are convinced about their own value.[79]

The Native American Women's Health Center incorporates another approach to the condom problem. In addition to building self-esteem, the center promotes condom distribution in reservation communities. Access to condoms through the center is particularly important because on the Yankton Sioux Reservation there is no twenty-four-hour convenience store where adolescents can buy condoms if they need them. In addressing this problem, the center encourages people in their workshops, and especially mothers, to get condoms from the pharmacy and IHS and distribute them freely. They suggest that they also "take a card and post it by the toilet or mirror saying that condoms are in the drawer or in the medicine cabinet and to help themselves to a batch of them."[80] This is a creative means of addressing access to and use of condoms. It is anonymous, there is no embarrassment or shame, and the condoms are easily accessible.

Many programs have been developed specifically to speak to kids; one that has worked well and has become entrenched in a variety of Native organizations is theater. Participating in youth theater is believed to be "conducive to effecting positive change in sexual behaviors and negotiation behaviors for safer sex" by giving participants experiential opportunities to practice communication and negotiation skills.[81] Theater work utilized by general AIDS organizations and groups has been extended to tribal communities. For example, the South-central Foundation AIDS Education and Personal Choices in Anchorage, Alaska, which serves Native Alaskans, created a puppet theater using Alaskan legends. Other agencies, such as the American Indian Community House in New York and the Minnesota American Indian AIDS Task Force, utilize theater as a form of prevention and youth empowerment.[82]

Creative peer-run events are another empowerment approach that works for adolescents. Messages are more accessible and credible when teens and young adults hear the contemporary vernacular provided by peer educators. Both the American Indian Community House and the Minnesota Indian Task Force utilize peer educators in their HIV/AIDS work. The American Indian Community House has an Outreach Education Coordinator Network (OEC), a program designed to empower and assist Native American communities to address the issues of HIV/AIDS openly and to develop culturally relevant outreach, education, and referral services. They have outreach sites in Buffalo, Akwesasne, Long Island, Syracuse/Onondaga, and New York City. These five sites have incorporated the use of peer educators, but they create prevention materials specific to their tribal cultures. For example, the off-reservation Erie and Niagara Native communities developed "the first ever Iroquois relevant HIV prevention curriculum for 9–13 year old youth" as well as using their youth to present the information locally.[83] At the November 1999 United States Conference on AIDS, held in Denver, the Akwesasne site sent their youth education coordinator, Kakwireiosta (Leyosta) Hall, to participate in the forum Native America in the Next Century: The Future Navigated by Youth and to share her insights about working on HIV/AIDS issues and Native youth.[84] Leyosta has participated in peer education for several years, and at the conference she shared her story of performing in an Akwesasne live youth play for fifty community members.[85]

Peer counselors have a very difficult job, but Native youth are facing the challenge with dignity and hope. Some young volunteers find their jobs difficult because of the stigma attached to AIDS. Others have discussed how people sometimes confront them about being HIV/AIDS positive (whether they are or not) and how they have to deal with fear and outrage. For example, Janice Wilson, a young Navajo peer counselor on the Navajo reservation, says that people become afraid of her and her family when they find out her father is HIV positive. She has been told horrible things, including that her father deserves to die, that it is God's way of punishing him, and that he ought to be locked up far away. Yet she endures and perseveres in her work to stop the spread of HIV/AIDS and to educate people about the disease.[86]

Finding good peer educators is equally difficult because the job invites suspicion that volunteers may carry the disease, and volunteers do not receive much support from their peers for their work.[87] Individual work is much more difficult than group work, where volunteers can gain strength from each other.

A sense of camaraderie can be found among the Minnesota American Indian AIDS Task Force's well-known theatrical group, The Ogitchidag Gikinoomaagad Players. The players are a group of Native youth dedicated to educating other youth and Native American communities about HIV/AIDS through storytelling, drama, music, and dance. Andrea Goze and Joy Rivera, participants in the Players, spoke at the Native America in the Next Century forum and told how important it was for them to help empower other youth. They also spoke of their experiences in developing and participating in educational prevention programs such as Human Bingo, K-6th Grade Puppet Shows, and Sexual Jeopardy. A quote used in their Youth Peer Education brochure demonstrates the solidarity of the group: "our group of actors are an example of our culture's strength. We are all from different tribes and backgrounds, but we pull together and unite, like the Native community does whenever there is a crisis."

A variety of Native organizations are confronting the difficult task of saving our children and youth. Focusing on the future of Native people, the American Indian Community House's Outreach Education Coordinator Network (OEC) chose the theme, "Children and Young People: Listen, Learn, and Live," to celebrate World AIDS Day, December 1999. The OEC Network in New York felt that "the theme reflects the fact that reaching out to children and young people is considered by many people to be the most promising strategy for reducing the spread of HIV worldwide."[88] On the other side of the nation, in November 1999, the National Native American

AIDS Prevention Center of California, sponsored the Native American Institute at the United States Conference on AIDS entitled Native America in the Next Century: The Future Navigated by Youth. This empowering session drew upon the wisdom of our Native youth in helping adult program designers develop and implement prevention and intervention programs for Native youth.

Concern about youth in isolated areas is a focus in Alaska, particularly in light of the state's youthful population. Youth aged fifteen to twenty-four represent 14 percent of the population of the United States, but 16 percent of the population in Alaska.[89] Fortunately there are a variety of agencies addressing the issues confronting these young people. One of them is the Alaska Area Native Health Services, part of IHS, which works with nine tribally operated service units in Alaska serving 110,000 Eskimos, Aleuts, and Indians. The services include tribal hospitals located in the six rural communities of Barrow, Bethel, Dillingham, Kotzebue, Nome, and Sitak, as well as twenty-two tribal health centers and seventy-four tribal community health aide clinics operated throughout the state.[90]

By law, the majority of services to Alaskan Natives are administered by the tribes themselves. The Yukon-Kuskokwin Health Corporation (YKHC) is one of several self-determining Native agencies. As a Native-run agency, it is addressing the needs of rural Alaska in a culturally sensitive manner. The YKHC, located in western Alaska, serves fifty Native villages in an area the size of the state of Washington. The villages are remote and hundreds of miles apart from each other, with populations ranging from thirty-seven to five thousand.[91] Each village has its own small clinic with several aides. They are faced with a challenging task in addressing the many health concerns facing Native Alaskan youth. In a recent Tribal Unity and Traditional Medicine gathering held at the Yupiit Piciryarait Cultural Center in April 1999, tribal elders, community members, and young people came to record their regional health care priorities and pass on traditional healing methods. At this gathering, the focus was on youth issues, and the young people were invited to participate in workshops and interact with elders, YKHC program directors, and board members. Alaskan youth also attended workshops on asset building, human immunodeficiency virus, and sexually transmitted diseases, alcohol and drugs, violence, inhalants, and suicide.[92] The connection between drug use and HIV has already been discussed in relation to other groups, but the connection is especially applicable to Alaskan Native females. A recent study found that there were "more Alaska Native injectors who were female than male . . . and a greater number of their sex partners are needle users."[93] This is important to know in creating HIV/AIDS prevention materials in Alaska.

In urban Alaska there are agencies that incorporate Native culture into their services. The Four A's, located in Anchorage, serves urban Natives, who were 23 percent of their client total in 1998.[94] With such a large percentage of Natives as clients, the agency makes a special effort to include messages directed toward them. In a recent newsletter on healing and spirituality, for example, they included a Native American prayer.[95] This organization is warm and welcoming to Natives. On a visit in 1999 I found their welcoming of Natives heartfelt and their services efficient.

In an effort to get the HIV/AIDS message out across Alaska, the Four A's have developed a Web site that "offers vital information on services to all Alaskans infected with HIV and links that provide up-to-the-minute prevention education."[96] Included in the site are links to Women and HIV/AIDS and Sites for Youth, as well as Ethnic HIV Information, which includes the National Native American AIDS Prevention Center and the Indian Health Service. One reason for developing the site was to give free and private access to HIV/AIDS information to youth and others.

Native youth program development and implementation is a daunting task in Alaska, in part, because of the isolation facing their youth. However, programs in Alaska confront the difficult task by joining together with other agencies, organizations, and programs.

The personnel shortages that hamper responses to the epidemic in rural America are especially relevant to Alaska. The U.S. National Commission on AIDS found that a lack of basic publicly supported services throughout rural America is hampering the nation's response to the HIV/AIDS epidemic. They also found a shortage of dentists, nurses, physicians, social workers, allied health workers, public health specialists, and volunteers willing to work with HIV/AIDS infected individuals. Shortages stemmed from a variety of reasons, including fear of occupational exposure, ignorance of the disease, lack of adequate training or expertise in treating HIV infections, and negative attitudes toward people from HIV risk groups. The commission recommended a comprehensive community-based primary health care system (supported by adequate funding and reimbursement rates); expansion of AIDS education and outreach services in rural communities designed to provide clear and direct messages about HIV; an increase and improvement of the effectiveness of all programs designed to educate and retain practicing health care professionals; creation of incentives for providers to care for people in underserved areas; and recognition and honoring of volunteers.[97]

When shortages of personnel are combined with issues of extreme isolation, as they are in Alaska, fighting the spread of HIV/AIDS, as well as treating and providing an adequate quality of life to those with AIDS, become almost insurmountable tasks. Isolation is a greater issue in Alaska than elsewhere in rural America. For example, providing mental health services to Alaskan Natives is exacerbated by "greater isolation, higher costs, and extreme weather conditions."[98] The same can be said about providing Native Alaskans with HIV/AIDS services. Transportation is itself a major challenge; indeed, some believe it to be the most critical issue confronting the Native health care system.[99] When a plane is the only way out of a Native village, transportation and its cost can place an incredible burden on an individual with HIV/AIDS.

The Alaska Native Health Board (ANHB), a twenty-two member entity established in 1968, is facing a multitude of health challenges. Regarded as the voice of Alaskan Natives, the ANHB represents the Alaska Federation of Natives and their health issues. The purpose of the ANHB is to promote the spiritual, physical, mental, social, and cultural well being and pride of Alaskan Native people. The ANHB meets quarterly to discuss health issues affecting all of Alaska's regions. At these meetings, health issues are identified and ranked, and then strategies are developed to address those issues. The ANHB receives funds from contracts and grants.

Working with a variety of agencies, the ANHB has advocated for community-based health care, improvements in health services, and adequate access to care. They serve as advisors to the Alaska Area Native Health Service, the U.S. Senate Committee on Indian Affairs, The House the Interior, and Insular Affairs Committee, and they work closely with the Alaska Department of Health and Social Services as well as state legislators.[100]

In their efforts to promote the well being of Native Alaskans, the ANHB has several ongoing programs, including the Rural Alaska Sanitation Coalition, the Epidemiology Program, the ANHB Trampling Tobacco Program, and a statewide HIV/AIDS Awareness Program. The ANHB AIDS Program, established in 1988, provides training, technical assistance, and educational materials that are distributed to the ANHB membership organizations.[101]

Through the dedication and hard work of the ANHB AIDS Program project manager Joe Cantil and AIDS training specialist Don Lemieux, the program works toward community empowerment and resource development. The training programs and skill building workshops address a variety of regional health organization issues related to rural concerns. The ANHB AIDS Program also acts as a clearing house for information on funding, training opportunities, and HIV/AIDS information and updates.[102]

To address health issues related to Native Alaskans, the program has created several HIV/AIDS educational videos. *I'm Not Afraid of Me* and *Kecia* are geared toward Natives in the North. *I'm Not Afraid of Me*, developed in part by the ANHB, tells the story of Barbara Byron, a young Native Alaskan woman who was infected heterosexually and then transmitted the disease to her daughter. This is a video about their personal journey. *Kecia* is a documentary about Kecia Larkin, a young Native girl from Vancouver Island. This video presents the events that led up to her becoming infected with HIV. Strong messages are given to young people about their bodies and HIV as the camera follows Kecia on a tour of Native communities. ANHB also sells Love Carefully merchandise and *Uncle Jake's Story*, a coloring book about two children who discover that their uncle Jake is HIV positive. This coloring book speaks to the youth of Alaska, as the uncle is shown living in a small rural Alaskan village.

Addressing the needs of Alaskan youth is critical for a variety of reasons. First, a study that examined hospital records from the Alaska Native Medical Center between 1980 and 1984 found that the suicide rate among Alaskan Natives was twice the national average. The study also found that the suicide rate for Native Alaskan youth, often associated with alcohol, was nine times the rate for all youth in the United States.[103] It is believed that the strong sense of hopelessness found among young Native Alaskans comes from disruption of their traditional lifestyles. Many Native Alaskan youth are faced with the drastic change from a subsistence lifestyle and are ill-prepared for modern life.[104] In an examination of suicide prevention programs for Alaskan Native youth, a regional state administrator found that there is a need to involve the youth in the development of prevention programs, as well as to garner a better understanding of what it means to serve a large isolated area.[105] These concerns should be taken into account in developing any prevention programs for rural Alaska.

ANHB has worked independently as well as jointly with other agencies in providing HIV/AIDS prevention, intervention, and education. In May 1999 the ANHB, together with YKHC, the Northwest AIDS Education and Training Center of the University of Washington, and the University of Alaska at Fairbanks, Kuskowkwim Campus, cosponsored an HIV/AIDS Clinical Update covering HIV/AIDS adherence strategies, multiple-diagnosed patients, services, testing, treatments, as well as stereotypes and fear in the family and community.[106]

Although Alaska faces some enormous challenges in its fight against HIV/AIDS, it falls upon all of us to appropriately address the needs of our youth. The AIDS epidemic is no longer a white gay man's problem; it is a world problem, crossing lines of ethnicity, gender, and age and "entrenching itself in the ranks of the poor and marginalized." [107] As we enter the twenty-first century, there is no prevention vaccine or cure for AIDS. So, to keep Native youth (who are often poor and marginalized) healthy, we must work toward developing and implementing comprehensive, skill-based, and developmentally and culturally appropriate health education programs both in schools and at sites that provide youth services. It is time to empower our children and to come together with various groups, agencies, organizations, and governments so that we can pool our resources in planning for the future of our Native children, tribes, villages, reservations, and urban communities.

# NATIVE AMERICAN PREVENTION

## Cultural Preservation and Survival

1    2    3    **4**

Native ability to endure and persevere has been demonstrated through-out history. For more than five hundred years Native peoples have con-fronted and surmounted oppressive policies and cultural disruption, as well as deadly diseases. The current challenge that HIV/AIDS presents is difficult, but not insurmountable. The fight against HIV/AIDS has been a long one, but if there is anything we have learned in the last twenty years, it is that pre-vention works. This knowledge was confirmed in 1994 by a research team from the University of California at San Francisco (UCSF), which found that "prevention programs can be effective in changing risk-taking behav-ior among participants and in decreasing the number of new HIV infec-tions over time."[1] To work effectively, however, these programs must not be static, and they must be developed with respect for and acknowledgment of differences in gender, class, age, and culture.

The need for HIV/AIDS prevention in Native America is vast because there are over five hundred tribes and villages nationwide, with a variety of languages, ceremonies, and social, political, and economic systems. Add to the diverse social and geographic conditions the necessity of addressing the unique needs of women, men, youth, and gays/bisexuals, and the task of developing effective programs can seem overwhelming. Creating culturally appropriate, gender-appropriate, and age-appropriate programs is easier to imagine than to do, especially if funding is a problem.

Repeating the history of inadequate funding for Native health problems, Native HIV/AIDS programs and prevention research have been poorly funded. One can only hope that HIV/AIDS prevention funding does not fol-low the history of lack of funding for smallpox, for example. When smallpox decimated whole tribes in the sixteenth century and continued to wreak havoc during the nineteenth century, very little treatment or prevention was undertaken due to a lack of money and interest. It was not until 1832 that Congress allocated funds to arrest the progress of smallpox among tribes. The funds were inadequate, however, and health care was frequently tied to

United States government and tribal relationships. In other words, small-pox vaccination was provided "as long as the Indians remained where the government claimed that they belong – on their reservations."[2] It was not until the 1860s that vaccinations succeeded in reducing Native American mortality rates from smallpox.[3] A 1995 study conducted by the UCSF team concluded that minority groups and young gay men have increasing HIV rates, yet prevention research in respect to minorities was limited.[4]

Funding for Native HIV/AIDS programs is also problematic since the number of Native AIDS infections is low compared to that of other racial groups. Although Native Americans were diagnosed in the early 1980s with AIDS, it was not until 1987–88 that the first Native American AIDS programs were funded, and it was not until 1989 that the Indian Health Service began a program addressing HIV/AIDS among tribal people.[5] Yet it is clear that HIV/AIDS rates are on the rise for people of color. Native Americans have many of the same "high-risk" factors as African American women, whose leading cause of death is now HIV/AIDS. In addition, HIV/AIDS is the eighth leading cause of death for Native Americans "between 15 and 34 living on or near reservations."[6] Thus it is important for those working with prevention fundraising to articulate clearly how critical it is to fund Native programs. Although many are complacent because of the drop in AIDS deaths, people are still at risk, and the problem is now even more serious among minority populations.

Today, many Native organizations and health officials lack the necessary funding to address the issue of AIDS. This concern was unanimously raised on 17 September 1997 in the HIV/AIDS Research and Evaluation in Native American Communities segment of the United States Conference on AIDS in Miami, Florida. At the conference the issue of funding was the center of all discussions in the Native workshops on evaluation, epidemiology, and needs assessments.[7] Funding was also the central concern of many organizations and individuals who participated in the United States Conference on AIDS in Denver in November 1999.

A major reason for the lack of funding is that AIDS money allocation is formula based; that is, the number of total cases reported is a major determining factor. Highest priority is given to programs for populations with the greatest need. As already noted, the total number of Native cases as of December 1999 is 2,132, less than 1 percent of all AIDS cases in the United States. An additional problem with funding for HIV/AIDS programs is an overall decrease in funding for Native health programs. In San Francisco, for example, health care reform resulted in the renegotiations of new contracts in 1994 that placed previously allotted Native American AIDS program monies in the hands of a broader program, the National Task Force on AIDS Prevention for People of Color. This action was met with resistance by several Native organizations that believe Native-run programs are more effective in addressing the needs of Native Americans because they consider the cultures and traditions of the various tribes.[8] Another important aspect to this argument is self-determination. Tribal people believe that each tribe should determine the implications of HIV/AIDS within its own communities, apply its own knowledge and experience in combating it, and be free to "realize its own vision of how an AIDS-free future might look."[9]

In 1996 the National Minority HIV Institute held a discussion on the impact of HIV in minority communities and developed recommendations for the federal government, hoping that the recommendations would be used to develop a national strategic plan for the development of culturally appropriate programs related to specific minority communities. The recommendations by the Native American component are telling. Basically, Native American recommendations included increased funding for Indian Health Service, community-based organizations, and interagency coordination for care and prevention.[10] The recommendations made in 1996 were followed by the 1999 Report to the Secretary for Minority Health calling for increased funding for the use of peers and mentors. The committee also recommended increased funding for urban Natives not covered by the Indian Health Service. They further suggested that the Health Resources and Services Administration (HRSA) and the Special Projects of National Significance Program (SPNS) review the Ryan White CARE Act to find a way to provide for ongoing funding for American Indian HIV/AIDS programs.[11]

The Ryan White CARE Act, which emanates from the Ryan White Comprehensive AIDS Resources Emergency Act of 1990 (Ryan White Act) and is administered by the HRSA, located within the U.S. Department of Health and Human Services, has been a much-needed source of funding for Native urban populations, but it is not without problems. The 1990 Ryan White Act was designed to provide emergency assistance to localities that are disproportionately affected by the HIV epidemic. It also gave financial assistance to states and other public or private nonprofit entities for the development, organization, coordination, and operation of more effective and cost-efficient systems for the delivery of essential services to individuals and families with HIV infection.[12] A problem with this act, addressed by Native American AIDS activists from 1993 to 1996, was that it provided financial assistance to states but not to tribes. Tribes, like states, are their own sovereigns, yet they are not listed as entities to receive funding.[13]

The Ryan White Act was amended and reauthorized in 1996 to revise and extend programs established in 1990.[14] Known as the Ryan White CARE Act, it consists of four titles and Part F (Special Projects of National Significance), that are administered by the HIV/AIDS Bureau of HRSA. The only place where the needs of Native people are addressed is in the SPNS section, which states that the "special projects of national significance shall include the development and assessment of innovative service delivery models that are designed to . . . ensure the ongoing availability of services for Native American communities to enable such communities to care for Native Americans with HIV disease."[15] One problem, however, is that the major focus is on service research and not service provision. Another problem is that Native people are one of six "special populations" vying for a small amount of money.

Several Native AIDS organizations and tribes have recently presented testimony to the HRSA AIDS Advisory Committee regarding the reauthorization of the Ryan White CARE Act. They recommend, in part, that a re-authorization must acknowledge the "existence of the federal trust responsibility toward tribal peoples and the existence of a Native health care system that is responsible for providing medical care . . . and insure funding for tribal and urban native health, mental health, and social service providers serving people with HIV/AIDS."[16] In addition, since Title II provides grants to states for health care and support services for persons with HIV/AIDS, tribes believe that the act should also specifically mention them since they too are sovereign entities and have a special relationship with the federal government. Furthermore, they recommend that the SPNS program be more sweeping in scope and "set-aside funds to pay for Native American care programs" specifically.[17]

At a time when public monies are spent on the basis of clout, Native Americans are faced with a daunting task, having neither large numbers nor strong unified political power. There has been a fear that since funding agencies are concerned with numbers, and infection rates for Natives are low at this time, "it is assumed that a certain number of Native Americans would have to die before funds for HIV prevention could be justified."[18] Rather than allow that to happen, Native organizations and tribes are collaborating in interagency, intergovernmental, and intertribal ventures. Self-determination is imperative for Natives in these ventures, however, because their own communities are being affected and self-determination must be understood in their own terms.

Although funding for HIV prevention and programs has not always flowed where it is needed (in this case prevention before the virus becomes an epidemic), Native health agencies, organizations, and programs persevere in their efforts to address HIV/AIDS needs and concerns. Realizing that prevention does work and that prevention programs need to address the unique needs of minority populations, Native people have worked independently and with others in creating culturally specific prevention strategies and programs. Developing and administering these programs have proven to be particularly difficult for tribal communities that are rural and isolated.[19]

Challenges aside, Native people endure and are confronting the rise of HIV/AIDS in culturally specific ways. However, very little literature can be found on the creation, implementation, and study of Native prevention strategies. What exists stresses the need for community input and participation, and consideration of Native spirituality and cultural values.[20] Being culturally specific is a necessary strategy for prevention to work in Native communities, but programs must also be expansive and include gender, age, sexual orientation, and specific community norms.[21]

The Institute for Health Policy Studies at UCSF has identified characteristics of HIV education and prevention that work. The characteristics are as follows: a clearly defined target population (i.e., age, gender, sexual orientation, race/ethnicity, neighborhood, and so forth); clearly defined objectives (i.e., what behaviors are being targeted for change, what new behaviors are to be achieved by whom); clearly defined interventions (i.e., intervention can be explained in simple terms); and targeting the highest-risk population, not just the easy-to-reach populations. In addition, the most effective strategies are programs that are "for, of, and by" the target populations. In essence, this means that Native people and in many cases Native leaders are involved in development and implementation and that the cultural and social context is shown to be true for the communities' individual experiences.[22]

Other characteristics of effective HIV/AIDS strategies include providing group support for individuals initiating and maintaining behavior changes; and enhancing individual self-esteem and providing concrete incentives to individuals. Effective strategies also draw on the spiritual resources and strengthen the spiritual life of individuals; use cultural resiliency factors to reach and empower the target population; work toward changing the physical and social environment of individuals; raise the visibility and lend support to HIV/AIDS prevention programs in the wider community; and reach people where they live, where they work, and where they go.

A critical aspect of Native HIV prevention is the use of multiple strategies that link to other components such as treatment, care, other disease prevention efforts, and that are tailored to meet the needs of people in different stages of the HIV/AIDS epidemic. Other aspects of a good program are a focus on achieving incremental changes over the long term; giving people something they want or need, rather than asking them to accept a new behavior or something they do not want; making the program site acceptable and accessible to the user; repeated and flexible interaction over time (that changes with the times); and linking alternative test sites and confidential test sites that target both HIV seronegatives and seropositives.[23]

As a means of sharing information relevant to prevention, the rest of the chapter lists various organizations and agencies that have implemented culturally specific Native American HIV/AIDS strategies. My hope is that these programs will serve as model projects for HIV/AIDS prevention among Native Americans and that they will be replicated by other agencies serving Native communities nationwide. In gathering this material I sent out surveys to Native AIDS organizations, agencies, and collaborative groups, asking them to share with me their most effective prevention strategy. The strategies presented demonstrate several important facts. One is that tribal groups are not homogenous. The needs of one tribal community are not the same as others. Another is that the strategies follow in part or in their entirety characteristics of HIV education and prevention programs that have been identified by researchers as successful.

Ahalaya Native Care Center, Inc.
1211 N. Shartel, Suite 404
Oklahoma City OK 73103


Ahalaya Project-Tulsa
3507 E. Admiral Place
Tulsa OK 74115
Contact: Vera Franklin

The Ahalaya Project, which has been in existence since November 1991, is a case management project designed for the local Native American community in Oklahoma to help meet the daily living, medical, personal, emotional, and psychosocial needs of Native Americans living with HIV. Its funding source is the Human Resource Services Administration's Special Projects of National Significance, through the National Native American AIDS Prevention Center (NNAAPC). The Ahalaya Project moved out of the umbrella of NNAAPC in February 2000. The objective of the Ahalaya Project is to stop the spread of HIV/AIDS and other sexually transmitted diseases among Native Americans by improving their health status through empowerment and self-determination. The project was developed to reach the Native American community by bridging the gap between non-Native educators and service providers.

The project is seen as successful because it is part of the Native American community and it measures all decisions, services, and care relative to the community it serves. In essence, it has redesigned service delivery to fit the culture. There are six components that all clients can access: traditional healing, referral services, essentials of life, health-oriented case management, secondary prevention services and social and psychological support. This project creates a bridge between health services provided by Indian Health Service and general community AIDS providers to ensure that Native clients have access to all essential services. The traditional healing component is reflective of a culturally specific program. This key component requires Ahalaya case managers to provide referrals to accepted traditional Native healers for healing. In addition, Ahalaya managers involve the healers in HIV/AIDS education programs.

Albuquerque Area Indian Health Board, Inc.
HIV/AIDS Prevention Program
2309 Renard Place, Suite 101
Albuquerque NM 87106

The Albuquerque Area Indian Health Board HIV/AIDS Prevention Program is a prevention and outreach project that serves urban and rural Native Americans in the state of New Mexico. The Prevention Program was established in 1989 and receives funding from both state and federal governments. The program's objectives are to provide education, training, service, and technical assistance to Albuquerque Area Indian Health Board tribes and technical assistance to other Indian Health Board tribes.

The board feels their most effective prevention strategy has been to mobilize the community using the Gathering of Native Americans Model, which targets both youth and adults. The model involves the community in identifying health problems and solutions that specifically address the impact that HIV infection may have in the community. The process includes community needs assessment to determine the specific needs of the community, data collection, program planning, identification of resources, implementation, and evaluation. Training services are developed at the request of the individual communities based on their health needs. The technical assistance consists of collaboration, sharing of resources, and providing recommendations to various agencies based on knowledge gained from community participants.

AICH Native American Outreach Education Coordinator Network
306 South Salina Street, Suite 201
Syracuse NY 13202
Contact: Cissy Elm

The Native American OEC Network is a program of the American Indian Community House (AICH) HIV/AIDS Project. AICH began in 1991 and is funded by the New York State Department of Health AIDS Institute. The OEC is designed to empower Native American communities throughout New York, assist them in openly addressing the issues of HIV/AIDS, and develop culturally relevant outreach, education, and referral services.

There are currently five outreach education coordinators, whose responsibilities include carrying out a risk reduction program to improve the health status of their community; promoting healthy behavior among Native Americans who are at risk within their community; providing HIV prevention education and referral services to Native Americans who seek out their assistance; and working on the development and maintenance of the Native American OEC Network within their local community. The five networks consist of ACT, NOW, Akwesasne OEC; AICH Sewanaka Place, Long Island OEC; Vision Quest, Buffalo OEC; Wish: Walk in Self-Harmony, Syracuse/Onondaga Nation OEC; and Manhattan OEC.

American Indian Community House HIV/AIDS Project
708 Broadway, 8th Floor
New York NY 10003
Contact: Cissy Elm

The American Indian Community House HIV/AIDS Project is part of the AICH Native American Outreach Education Coordinator Network, which serves New York. Their objectives are to increase the level of AIDS awareness among New York Native Americans and to provide culturally appropriate referral and case management services for Native Americans living with HIV/AIDS.

The most effective way of disseminating information to Native communities has been through Natives themselves. One of their most impressive programs is the Native American Generations Program. This project is an intergeneration approach used to provide community-based HIV prevention to Native American communities in central and northern New York State. The Generations Program trains Native American elders as HIV educators and then uses them to provide behavior-based primary HIV prevention education to Native American youth between the ages of twelve and twenty. The program also facilitates Native American youth production of HIV prevention public information to influence Native American community norms in support of safer behaviors.

Eagle Lodge Outpatient
2801 E. Colfax, Suite 306
Denver CO 80206
Contact: Geri Reyna

The Eagle Lodge serves six counties in the state of Colorado and is funded, in part, by the Indian Health Service. The program also joins with interstate compacts to provide a variety of services to Native American populations that need them. Joint efforts are a critical aspect of this program. The Eagle Lodge gets involved with a number of agencies such as hospitals, courts, schools, intervention programs, as well as tribal programs and courts to better serve tribal people. Their primary service consists of Native American substance abuse as well as HIV/AIDS prevention and intervention. They focus on the importance of family and work with adults and adolescents. The Eagle Lodge has utilized their support regularly for hospice care.

Their HIV/AIDS prevention program targets youth, including preschool and elementary-age children. To engage the kids they have lacrosse and UNITY programs. They work to make prevention messages fun and educational.

Fort Peck Tribe
Ft. Peck Tribal Health
PO Box 1027
Poplar MT 59255
Contact: Verbena Savior, Public Health Educator

The Ft. Peck Tribal Health Program serves the Fort Peck Reservation and is funded through the Montana State AIDS Project and the Northwest Portland Health Board. Its objectives include providing health resource services, transportation, vital statistics, and medical services to community members.

If an individual community member is diagnosed with HIV/AIDS he or she is referred to the Public Health Educator, who serves as a case manager and helps the client apply for Social Security Disability, housing, medication, and other needs. The Ft. Peck Tribal Health Program has an active HIV/AIDS policy, and AIDS coordinators who have had counseling training and are HIV/AIDS 101 instructor certified. In addressing the importance of education, they present HIV/AIDS information in high schools and on World AIDS Day, have HIV/AIDS poster contests in all the schools, and distribute "snag bags" with HIV/AIDS health materials at powwows.

Inter-Tribal Council of Arizona – HIV/STD Program
2214 North Central, Suite 100
Phoenix AZ 85004
Contact: Armando L. Gonzales, Project Training Coordinator

The Inter-Tribal Council of Arizona HIV/STD Program's objective is to serve the needs of tribal governments in Arizona, Utah, and Nevada. Funding for this program is provided by the Centers for Disease Control and Prevention. Pursuant to the request and needs of the tribal governments, the Inter-Tribal Council offers Native American-specific, culturally sensitive training to forty-two tribes within Arizona, Utah, and Nevada. The training and technical assistance to the various tribes is based on HIV/STD/ AIDS prevention education and incorporates a Native American focus in all age and gender categories.

Ke Ola Mamo
1130 N. Nimitz, Suite A–221
Honolulu HI 96817
Contact: Carol Odo

Ke Ola Mamo is a health education and prevention program that serves Native Hawaiians living in Oahu, Hawaii. Their funding sources have included the Bureau of Public Health Care, Centers for Disease Control, the State of Hawaii, as well as private foundations. Ke Ola Mamo's objectives are to raise community awareness of HIV and to reduce the risk of HIV infection among men who have sex with men in their specific target group – Native Hawaiians between eighteen and forty years of age. Ke Ola Mamo has found that individual-level intervention, counseling, and referral to health and social services has been most effective if peer staff are involved. They believe that peer staff are key to all interventions.

One of the most creative projects sponsored by the Ke Ola Mamo's Lei Anuenue HIV Prevention Program is the Lei Anuenue Retreat for transgenders. The primary goal at Lei Anuenue is to empower the young and old by giving them the skills and knowledge to improve and maintain healthy lifestyles. Empowering themselves includes community building, which entails self-education and educating their families and communities about transgender issues. At the retreat participants learn and practice behaviors that promote their health and well being, including STD/HIV prevention methods and harm-reduction tactics. At the retreat they try to maintain pono (balance) in their ola (life) as their ancestors did.

Minnesota American Indian AIDS Task Force
1433 E. Franklin Ave., Suite 19
Minneapolis MN 55404
Contact: Sharon Day, Director

The Minnesota American Indian AIDS Task Force (MAIATF) is an AIDS service organization that provides case management for people living with AIDS and health education and prevention programs for those living primarily in Minnesota. Funding sources include the state, foundations, and corporations. The mission of the MAIATF is to provide education and prevention outreach to prevent the spread of HIV among Native Americans and to provide direct services to Native Americans living with HIV and their families.

MAIATF contends that, of all the services they provide, their most effective culturally specific prevention program is their Ogitchidag Gikinooamaagad (Ojibway word that means warrior/teacher) Peer Education Program for Youth. Primarily for Native youth, this program contains a health education curriculum complete with skills training such as role playing. The topics covered include AIDS 101, cultural identity, heroes, teen pregnancy, alcohol and drug prevention, violence prevention, and sexually transmitted diseases. The youth also learn acting skills, which they can use to perform culturally specific plays for other youth (their peers) about these topics. The youth in the program are paid minimum wage and are given a stipend for performing plays. Art therapy is another component of the program. In a recent evaluation report, the Ogitchidag Gikinooamaagad Peer Education Program for Youth has been shown to be effective in achieving impacts on the high-risk target population, and in reaching more people in the Native community with important information about HIV/AIDS.

Montana United Indian Association
PO Box 6043
515 N. Saunders
Helena MT 59604
Contact: Patricia Maki

The Montana United Indian Association is a job training partnership program that does outreach and provides case management, counseling, financial assistance, and support services for those entering employment. The program serves all of the state of Montana minus the Indian reservations. The program objective is to better the lives of Indian people living in urban areas of Montana by using a holistic approach through case management. Their target groups include Native Americans in high school through retirement, males and females, and "at risk" and "hard-to-serve" Natives – those who live below the poverty level, are undereducated and underserved.

The Montana United Indian Association found that working collaboratively with the Urban Indian Centers to be effective in providing AIDS information to clients. The association also developed an AIDS manual, *Train the Trainers.* Urban Indian Centers' staff and volunteers were trained to train Native community members to provide AIDS prevention to their own communities.

National Native American AIDS Prevention Center
436 14th Street, Suite 1020
Oakland CA 94612
Contact: Ron Rowell, Executive Director

NNAAPC's services are national and include capacity-building technical assistance (organizational development, grantsmanship, resource development), case management for Native people with HIV/AIDS, research, and public policy. Their mission is to stop the spread of HIV and related diseases among American Indians, Alaskan Natives and Native Hawaiians, and to improve the quality of life of those infected and affected in Native communities. NNAAPC funding sources include the Centers for Disease Control and Prevention, the Health Resources and Services Administration, the Ford Foundation, the Gill Foundation, the Silva-Moonwalk Fund, and various other corporate donors.

NNAAPC believes that the most effective culturally specific prevention strategies are those that involve building community. For gay/bisexual/two-spirit native men, the group most affected by HIV thus far, they believe the best strategies are to create social alternatives to bars, to integrate gay/bisexual/two-spirit Native men and women into the greater Native cultural community, and to focus on the positive. For intravenous drug users, they feel the most effective approaches are both harm reduction (education about sharing needles, needle exchange, bleach kits) and having treatment available on demand. For Native women, who are increasingly infected by heterosexual transmission of HIV, there is a need for a more diverse prevention approach that deals with the realities of their lives. NNAAPC incorporates programs that address women who have been infected through sex with IV drug users and bisexuals, and those who have been involved in abusive relationships.

In conclusion, NNAAPC strongly stresses the importance of targeting HIV prevention programs to those at most risk based upon the epidemiological evidence. The approach differs according to the at-risk population in question, since, for example the difficulties facing gay/bisexual/two-spirit men are not necessarily those of intravenous drug users or their sexual partners.

Native American Community Services of Erie and Niagara Counties
1005 Grant Street
Buffalo NY 14207
PO Box 2161
561 Portage Road #329
Niagara Falls NY 14301
Contact: Norine Borkowski, Director of Education and Prevention

The Native American Community Services is a nonprofit human service provider serving Erie and Niagara counties. Funding is provided by federal, state, county, and city agencies as well as by United Way and private foundations. The agency's mission is to meet the social and economic needs of the off-reservation Native American community in Erie and Niagara counties.

They feel their most effective prevention service is aimed at Native youth from ages five to twenty. They provide a Youth Development Program consisting of case management, prevention workshops, and group activities that include cultural crafts, social events, and special field trips. Once a year they have a youth design project to educate the community about the effects of drugs, alcohol, and to enhance HIV/AIDS awareness. The youth create culturally relevant designs with a provocative message for Native Americans living in New York State and Southern Ontario province. The goal of the youth services is to forestall high-risk behavior and assist in modifying current behavior by encouraging Native American youth to participate in health maintenance activities.

Native American Health Center
56 Julian Avenue
San Francisco CA 94103
Contact: Parousha Zand

The Native American Health Center serves the San Francisco Bay area and is a community full health center. It receives funding from Ryan White CARE, Title I and II, and Indian Health Service. The center's mission is to assist American Indians and Alaskan Natives to improve and maintain their physical, mental, emotional, social and spiritual well-being with respect for cultural traditions, and to advocate for the needs of all Indian people, especially the most vulnerable members of that community.

Their most effective program is to provide integrated services to Natives living with HIV/AIDS through a multidisciplinary team utilizing a nurse case manager as the main coordinator along with a treatment advocate and a peer advocate. Services include primary care, dental services, mental health, and medication adherence. The center advocates prevention through assisting clients to choose safer behaviors and providing support and social activities. They use a variety of incentives to get potential clients involved in the center. For example, they provide free tickets to lesbian/gay films.

Native American Health/AIDS Coalition
6025 Prospect, Suite 103
Kansas City MO 64130
Contact: JG GoodTracks

The Native American Health/AIDS Coalition of Kansas and Missouri has implemented a collaborative team consisting of reservation and urban organizations designed to work with Native American HIV/AIDS issues in both states. Funding sources include the Ryan White CARE Act, Ahalaya funds from Oklahoma, and various forms of "in-kind" support. The project goals include collecting accurate Native HIV/AIDS data for Kansas and Missouri, reviewing and correcting HIV/AIDS mortality data from Kansas and Missouri to determine the accuracy of racial classification, and developing and implementing culturally relevant HIV/AIDS programs.

To collect accurate data, the coalition, along with four federal reservation and urban Indian organizations, developed and implemented a needs assessment survey. From the needs survey the coalition was able to plan, develop, and implement a culturally competent case management program for the service community. The second goal of data collection is ongoing and is achieved through active collaboration with the State Department of Health. As a result, the coalition has found twenty-four misclassified Native cases and a total of fifty-four Native HIV/AIDS cases in Kansas and Missouri combined.

The coalition continues to have success with their third goal, in part because of strong partnerships developed among tribal nations and urban HIV/AIDS organizations. Through the use of needs assessment they have been able to plan, develop, and implement a culturally competent case management program for each respective community. The coalition also provides confidential services for HIV positive Native and non-Native

Americans, including, but not limited to, the use of Native American case managers, counseling, anonymous HIV/AIDS testing, housing and food referrals, Native American support groups, cultural and spiritual resources, urban and reservation outreach, and culturally sensitive education for health and AIDS service organizations.

Northern Cheyenne Board of Health
Health Education and Tribal Health
PO Box 67
Lame Deer MT 59043
Contact: Lee Ann Bruised Head

The Northern Cheyenne Board of Health's Public Health Education-Outreach Program serves the needs of those located within the Northern Cheyenne Reservation. The program objectives are to ensure quality in community-based health and wellness services, as well as to encourage, support, and empower the community. In addition, they are required to support health programs and services that best represent the Northern Cheyenne way of life.

Their most effective prevention strategies, aimed at Cheyenne youth, include a Native presenter of educational materials and use of a culturally specific Planned Parenthood video (set at a powwow) that addresses drinking, STDs, and teen pregnancy. The Education-Outreach Program also provides information on HIV/AIDS prevention at local powwows.

A major concern of the program is early teen sexual exploration and experimentation. Hence, the program is designed so that health care providers clarify the understanding of the basic need for touch versus sexual touch and work toward promoting hugs, kisses, and cuddles without sexual risk.

Papa Ola Lokahi
222 Merchant St., 2nd Floor
Honolulu HI 96813
Contact: Pua Aiu

Papa Ola Lokahi (POL) was created by the Native Hawaiian Health Care Improvement Act of 1988 to provide technical support and administrative assistance to Native Hawaiians. The geographic area served is the state of Hawaii. POL receives federal and NNAAPC funding and its mission is to "improve the health status of Native Hawaiians by advocating, initiating, and maintaining culturally appropriate strategic actions aimed at improving the physical, mental, and spiritual health of Native Hawaiians." POL is also mandated to do demonstration projects and to establish planning networks to ensure the proper care of Native Hawaiians throughout the state.

One project is the AIDS Case Management Program. Based on the data collected, POL develops a culturally competent case management program that addresses Native Hawaii HIV/AIDS needs. The case management program serves O'ahu and Maui. What POL finds to be essential in providing culturally appropriate assistance is the hiring of the "right" case manager, one who is aware of and part of the Hawaiian culture and is compassionate and understanding.

Salish Kootenai Tribe
Tribal Health and Human Services
PO Box 280
St. Ignatius MT 59865
Contact: Sandra Sorrell or Wendy Duran

The Salish Kootenai Tribal Health Department serves the Flathead Reservation in northwestern Montana and is funded by the state, the Centers for Disease Control HIV Grant, and Indian Health Service. The objectives of the department are to prevent the spread of HIV in Indian Country.

One of the programs is focused on the inmate population. Recently, the Salish Kootenai Tribal Health Department held focus groups on HIV education and prevention in their tribal jail. They gathered information on educational strategies and intravenous drug culture, and had the inmates help develop culturally specific educational materials that they thought would work.

An outcome of the focus groups was the development of an informational gift package given to new inmates that includes toothbrushes, HIV/HCV/STD/IDU brochures, playing cards with drug education information, resource lists, microwave popcorn, and a soda. They also developed exit packages that include the same materials as well as condoms, bleach kits, and money for a phone call. The Salish Kootenai Tribal Health Department also provides in-jail educational games, an HIV video pizza night, and an HIV/AIDS educational popcorn party.

Spirit Lake Sioux Tribe
Health Education Program
Tribal Health Office
398 Fort Totten ND 58335
Contact: Duane Guy

The Spirit Lake Sioux Tribal Health Education Program serves four districts within the Spirit Lake Sioux Reservation. Presently, the Health Education Program is working without outside funding to address the needs of HIV/AIDS clients. They have, however, combined prevention efforts with another program aimed at reducing the number of pregnancies of young tribal women. This program uses Native women to talk to young mothers (ages fifteen to twenty-four) about sex, diseases, and goal setting. The women discuss the importance of safe sex and stress that sex is not always the way to tell your partner that you love him. The program stresses that it is extremely important to let young parents know what their responsibilities are in order to be safe and healthy.

Two-Spirit Society
PO Box 7523
Boulder CO 80306–7523
Contact: David Young

The Two-Spirit Society is a spiritual group for two-spirit people. The geographic area it serves is Turtle Island. It obtains funding from the Gill Foundation, and the Dextra Baldwin McGonagle Foundation, Inc., and receives personal contributions from members of the local community. The organization's objectives are to advocate a sober, healthy, spiritual lifestyle. It is dedicated to the preservation of indigenous culture practiced prior to the arrival of peoples from the Eastern Hemisphere.

Members feel their most promising HIV/AIDS prevention strategy is to mend the Sacred Hoop through prayer and to practice traditional ways in contemporary society. They teach two-spirit individuals to walk the Red Road and return to their communities to heal the injuries done by five centuries of European thought and exploitation. They fulfill part of their mission by sponsoring a two-spirit camp once a year and by sharing two-spirit experiences with elders. They ask elders to help teach their respective communities about two-spirit issues and HIV/AIDS. They feel strongly that tribal communities will not find solutions to their problems through the bureaucratic process of a system that exploits all things for domination and profit. In contrast, they believe that their ancestors provided them with all of the tools they need to heal themselves, their communities, and the world of two-legged beings. If they choose to ignore the teachings of their elders, they believe they have no one to blame but themselves: "Whatever the losses, whatever the gains, they are yours." It is at the two-spirit camps where they learn to connect with the teachings of the past.

Walking the Wellness Path
HIV/AIDS Program
Indian Health Board of Minneapolis
1315 E. 24th Street
Minneapolis MN 55404
Contact: Jacquelyn Farrow

Walking the Wellness Path is a program located within the Indian Health Board of Minneapolis and provides outreach, case management, and education primarily to the inner city but also has outreach links to surrounding areas. Walking the Wellness Path is funded through the Ryan White CARE Act, Indian Health Service, and private donations. The program's primary purpose is to stop the transmission of HIV/AIDS as well as to provide compassionate and comprehensive advocacy services and care to Native American community members living with HIV/AIDS. This advocacy (case management) includes family and friends.

One of the most effective services is having the case managers go to the clients. They meet people where they feel most comfortable, and then they help them obtain what they want or need (i.e., to visit with a spiritual healer, attend a sacred pipe ceremony). The case managers are aware that nobody can deal with HIV/AIDS until some basic needs are met. What makes this program unique is that case managers work with people to meet all of their needs, and not just those that seem directly connected to HIV/AIDS. This particular service attempts to target people who have slipped through other programs and have no other resources.

Winnebago Healthy Start
PO Box 3704
Sioux City IA 51102
Contact: Deb Scholten, Executive Director

Winnebago Healthy Start is a case management program for Native Americans that serves the Winnebago Reservation, Iowa's Woodbury County, and Dakota County in northeast Nebraska. The program is funded by the Centers for Disease Control and the Community Based Organizations HIV Prevention Coop-Agreement. The objectives of the Winnebago Healthy Start Program are to reduce high-risk behaviors (i.e., intravenous drug use, multiple sexual partners, and so on) and replace them with healthy lifestyles that reinforce traditional values.

Winnebago Healthy Start provides several effective prevention strategies, including the dissemination of HIV/AIDS information through home visits with pregnant women and new mothers and its involvement in the AA Recovery Program/Talking Circle. In addition, they utilize an interactive CD, culturally specific to Winnebagos, which focuses on the importance of HIV prevention to the future of the tribe.

Yukon Kuskokwim Health Corporation
Attn: Health Education
PO Box 528
Bethel AK 99559
Contact: Patrice Walrod

The Yukon Health Corporation, a federally and state funded nonprofit organization, has created a tribal health consortium that provides inpatient and ambulatory services, primary care, and preventive and health protection services in the Yukon Kuskokwim Delta region in Alaska. The mission of the tribal health consortium is to achieve the greatest possible improvement in the health status of the people of the Yukon-Kuskokwim Delta region. In addition, it is committed to the development of culturally relevant programs for primary care, prevention, and health promotion in a setting that fosters Native self-determination in the control and management of health delivery.

The consortium's most effective prevention strategy entails providing opportunities to learn and discuss HIV/AIDS prevention at presentations, as well as using guest speakers at community events. Tribal presenters are used as much as possible to speak to Native Alaskans. The presenters are also required to address critical issues, such as substance abuse, since it is a problem in many of the Native villages, as well as a high-risk behavior in the spread of HIV/AIDS.

# RESOURCE GUIDE

This guide lists resources in the following categories: Native American AIDS Videos, Organizations and Tribal Health Offices, Other Organizations, Annual Conferences, and Web Sites

## NATIVE AMERICAN AIDS VIDEOS

*AIDS: American Indians Dying Silently.* Produced and directed by Conrad and Nichols, Ltd. 10 min. New Mexico AIDS Prevention Program, Public Health Division. Videocassette.

*AIDS and the Native American Family.* Produced by Upstream Productions. Directed by Sandra Osawa. 11 min. Los Angeles County AIDS Program Office, 1990. Videocassette.

*AIDS in the Circle of Life.* Produced by J. Rolf. 20 min. Northern Arizona University, Johns Hopkins AIDS Prevention Project and the Native American Prevention Project against AIDS and Substance Abuse. Collaboration with Navajo and Hopi Nation reservations and border town schools and communities, 1992. Videocassette.

*AIDS Is Here.* Produced by J. Rolf. Northern Arizona University, Johns Hopkins AIDS Prevention Project and the Native American Prevention Project against AIDS and Substance Abuse. Collaboration with Navajo and Hopi Nation reservations and border town schools and communities, 1991. Videocassette.

*AIDS Is Your Business.* Produced by J. Rolf. 18 min. Northern Arizona University, Johns Hopkins AIDS Prevention Project and the Native American Prevention Project against AIDS and Substance Abuse. Collaboration with Navajo and Hopi Nation reservations and border town schools and communities. Star Video Duplicating, 1992. Videocassette.

*AIDS on Navajo Land: One Family Story.* Produced by J. Rolf. 30 min. Northern Arizona University, Johns Hopkins AIDS Prevention Project and the Native American Prevention Project against AIDS and Substance Abuse. Collaboration with

Navajo and Hopi Nation reservations and border town schools and communities. Star Video Duplicating, 1992. Videocassette.

*AIDS . . . Transmission and Prevention.* Produced by J. Rolf. 8 min. Northern Arizona University, Johns Hopkins AIDS Prevention Project and the Native American Prevention Project against AIDS and Substance Abuse. Star Video Duplicating, 1994. Videocassette.

*American Indians against HIV/AIDS Leadership Project.* Produced by KAT Productions. 17 min. University of North Dakota Department of Family Medicine, 1991. Videocassette.

*American Indians against HIV/AIDS Leadership Project: Presentation by Carole Lafavor.* 40 min. University of North Dakota Department of Family Medicine, 1991. Videocassette.

*American Indians against HIV/AIDS Leadership Project: Presentation by John Bird.* 120 min. University of North Dakota Department of Family Medicine, 1991. Videocassette.

*American Indians against HIV/AIDS Leadership Project: Presentation by Martin Broken Leg.* 126 min. University of North Dakota Department of Family Medicine, 1991. Videocassette.

*At the Edge . . . Arizona at Risk.* Produced by J. Rolf. 21 min. Northern Arizona University, Johns Hopkins AIDS Prevention Project and the Native American Prevention Project against AIDS and Substance Abuse. Star Video Duplicating. Videocassette.

*AZ Safe AZ Possible.* Produced by J. Rolf. 63 min. Northern Arizona University, Johns Hopkins AIDS Prevention Project and the Native American Prevention Project against AIDS and Substance Abuse. Collaboration with Navajo and Hopi Nation reservations and border town schools and communities, 1992. Videocassette.

*A Chance for Change.* Produced by Gryphon Productions, Ltd. Directed by Peter von Puttkamer. 31 min. Nuu-chan-nulth Health Board, Deptartment of National Health and Welfare and Province of British Columbia Ministry of Health, 1990. Videocassette.

*Choices.* Produced by J. Rolf. 13 min. Northern Arizona University, Johns Hopkins AIDS Prevention Project and the Native American Prevention Project against AIDS and Substance Abuse. Star Video Duplicating, 1994. Videocassette.

*Circle of Life.* Produced by Planned Parenthood of Central Oklahoma. 11 min. 1993. Videocassette.

*Circle of Warriors.* Produced by Phil Lucas Productions. Directed by Phil Lucas. 27 min. National Native American AIDS Prevention Center, 1989. Videocassette.

*Culture: Our Source of Values.* Produced by J. Rolf. 20 min. Northern Arizona University, Johns Hopkins AIDS Prevention Project and the Native American Prevention Project against AIDS and Substance Abuse. Star Video Duplicating, 1995. Videocassette.

*Face to Face: Native Americans Living with the AIDS Virus.* Produced by Phil Lucas Productions. Directed by Phil Lucas. 45 min. Rural Alaska Community Action Program and Alaska Native Health Board, 1989. Videocassette.

*A Father's Love.* Produced by J. Rolf. 21 min. Northern Arizona University, Johns Hopkins AIDS Prevention Project and the Native American Prevention Project against AIDS and Substance Abuse. Star Video Duplicating, 1995. Videocassette.

*Fighting for Our Lives: Women Confronting AIDS.* Produced by Center for Women's Policy Studies, Washington DC, and Anguiano Productions. Directed by Gail Harris and Kathleen Stol. 29 min. 1990. Videocassette.

*Her Giveaway: A Spiritual Journey with AIDS.* Produced by Skyman-Smith. Directed by Mona Smith. 22 min. Women Make Movies, New York, 1987. Videocassette.

*HIV/AIDS: A Threat to Our People, the Three Affiliated Tribes of the Fort Berthold Reservation.* Produced by KAT Video Productions. 16 min. University of North Dakota School of Medicine and the Three Affiliated Tribes, 1991. Videocassette.

*I'm Not Afraid of Me.* Produced by Phil Lucas Productions. Directed by Phil Lucas. 29 min. Alaska Native Health Board, 1991. Videocassette.

*Insights on HIV/AIDS: Native Children to Children.* Produced by Rosenda Reins Production. Directed by Beverly Singer. 15 min. 1997. Videocassette.

*Instructor's Training for the S.O.D.A.S. Skill Building Techniques.* Produced by J. Rolf. 30 min. Northern Arizona University, Johns Hopkins AIDS Prevention Project and the Native American Prevention Project against AIDS and Substance Abuse. Collaboration with Navajo and Hopi Nation reservations and border town schools and communities, 1992. Videocassette.

*An Interruption in the Journey.* Produced by Skyman-Smith. Directed by Mona Smith. 20 min. Minnesota AIDS Funding Consortium, 1991. Videocassette.

*It Can Happen to Anybody.* Produced and directed by Charles Abourezk. 22 min. Native American Women's Health Education Resource Center, 1990. Videocassette.

*It's Up to You.* Produced by J. Rolf. 15 min. Northern Arizona University, Johns Hopkins AIDS Prevention Project and the Native American Prevention Project against AIDS and Substance Abuse. Collaboration with Navajo and Hopi Nation reservations and border town schools and communities, 1991. Videocassette.

*Living Safe: Knowing About AIDS.* Produced by Tri-Video, Ltd. Directed by Herman Hastings and Clarence Wald. 16 min. Devil's Lake Sioux Tribe, 1989. Videocassette.

*Making It Happen: American Indians and HIV/AIDS Education.* Produced by American Red Cross. 1993. Videocassette.

*Michelle's Story.* Produced by J. Rolf. 23 min. Northern Arizona University, Johns Hopkins AIDS Prevention Project and the Native American Prevention Project against AIDS and Substance Abuse. Star Video Duplicating, 1995. Videocassette.

*Mom and Sons Series.* Produced by Circle Eagle Communications. 14:33 min. Native American Women's Health Education Resource Center, 1991. Videocassette.

*NAPPASA-Southwest Partners for Prevention.* Produced by J. Rolf. 28 min. Northern Arizona University, Johns Hopkins AIDS Prevention Project and the Native American Prevention Project against AIDS and Substance Abuse. Collaboration with Navajo and Hopi Nation reservations and border town schools and communities, 1994. Videocassette.

*Navajo AIDS Panel.* Produced by J. Rolf. 26 min. Northern Arizona University, Johns Hopkins AIDS Prevention Project and the Native American Prevention Project against AIDS and Substance Abuse. Star Video Duplicating, 1992. Videocassette.

*A Navajo Panel Discussion about HIV/AIDS.* Produced by J. Rolf. 26 min. Northern Arizona University, Johns Hopkins AIDS Prevention Project and the Native American Prevention Project against AIDS and Substance Abuse. Collaboration with Navajo and Hopi Nation reservations and border town schools and communities, 1992. Videocassette.

*New Challenges for Parents.* Produced by J. Rolf. 12 min. Northern Arizona University, Johns Hopkins AIDS Prevention Project and the Native American Prevention Project against AIDS and Substance Abuse. Collaboration with Navajo and Hopi Nation reservations and border town schools and communities, 1991. Videocassette.

*Not a Nice Way to Die.* Produced by J. Rolf. 11 min. Northern Arizona University, Johns Hopkins AIDS Prevention Project and the Native American Prevention Project against AIDS and Substance Abuse. Star Video Duplicating, 1994. Videocassette.

*Not to Worry.* Produced by J. Rolf. 20 min. Northern Arizona University, Johns Hopkins AIDS Prevention Project and the Native American Prevention Project against AIDS and Substance Abuse. Collaboration with Navajo and Hopi Nation reservations and border town schools and communities, 1992. Videocassette.

*Plans for Being Two: AIDS Information for Senior High School.* Produced by Tri-Video, Ltd. Directed by Herman Hastings and Clarence Wald. 21 min. Standing Rock Sioux Tribe, 1989. Videocassette.

*Pressures.* Produced by J. Rolf. 20 min. Northern Arizona University, Johns Hopkins AIDS Prevention Project and the Native American Prevention Project against AIDS and Substance Abuse. Collaboration with Navajo and Hopi Nation reservations and border town schools and communities, 1990–92. Videocassette.

*Road Trip.* Produced by J. Rolf. 13 min. Northern Arizona University, Johns Hopkins AIDS Prevention Project and the Native American Prevention Project against

AIDS and Substance Abuse. Collaboration with Navajo and Hopi Nation reservations and border town schools and communities, 1997. Videocassette.

*Sharing the Prevention Vision.* Produced by J. Rolf. 15 min. Northern Arizona University, Johns Hopkins AIDS Prevention Project and the Native American Prevention Project against AIDS and Substance Abuse. Collaboration with Navajo and Hopi Nation reservations and border town schools and communities. Star Video Duplicating, 1994. Videocassette.

*SODAS! How it Works.* Produced by J. Rolf. 5 min. Northern Arizona University, Johns Hopkins AIDS Prevention Project and the Native American Prevention Project against AIDS and Substance Abuse. Star Video Duplicating, 1994. Videocassette.

*SODAS Demonstration.* Produced by J. Rolf. 5 min. Northern Arizona University, Johns Hopkins AIDS Prevention Project and the Native American Prevention Project against AIDS and Substance Abuse. Star Video Duplicating, 1995. Videocassette.

*Taking Care of Yourself and Your Partner.* Produced by J. Rolf. 13 min. Northern Arizona University, Johns Hopkins AIDS Prevention Project and the Native American Prevention Project against AIDS and Substance Abuse. Collaboration with Navajo and Hopi Nation reservations and border town schools and communities, 1991. Videocassette.

*A Traditional Kind of Woman: Too Much and Not 'Nuff.* Directed by Richard Lance. 45 min. American Indian Community House, 1998. Videocassette.

*Values . . . What, When and How?* Produced by J. Rolf. 19 min. Northern Arizona University, Johns Hopkins AIDS Prevention Project and the Native American Prevention Project against AIDS and Substance Abuse. Star Video Duplicating, 1994. Videocassette.

Vernon, Irene. *Native American AIDS Video Resource Manual.* Colorado: Tri-Ethnic Center for Prevention Research, 1999.

*We Owe It to Ourselves and to Our Children.* Produced and Directed by the Human Health Organization in cooperation with the National Native American AIDS Prevention Center. 8 min. National Native American AIDS Prevention Center, 1989. Videocassette.

*What They Have to Say.* Produced by J. Rolf. 20 min. Northern Arizona University, Johns Hopkins AIDS Prevention Project and the Native American Prevention Project against AIDS and Substance Abuse. Collaboration with Navajo and Hopi Nation reservations and border town schools and communities, 1992. Videocassette.

*Who Can I Talk To?* Produced by J. Rolf. 12 min. Northern Arizona University, Johns Hopkins AIDS Prevention Project and the Native American Prevention Project against AIDS and Substance Abuse. Star Video Duplicating, 1995. Videocassette.

*Winslow High School HIV/AIDS Panel.* Produced by J. Rolf. 35 min. Northern Arizona University, Johns Hopkins AIDS Prevention Project and the Native American Prevention Project against AIDS and Substance Abuse. Collaboration with Navajo and Hopi Nation reservations and border town schools and communities. Star Video Duplicating, 1992. Videocassette.

ORGANIZATIONS AND TRIBAL HEALTH OFFICES

*Alaska*

Alaska Native Health Board HIV/AIDS Project, 4201 Tudor Center, Suite 105, Anchorage AK 99508. Tel: (907) 562–6006.
Chugachmiut, 4201 Tudor Center Drive, Suite 210, Anchorage AK 99508. Tel: (907) 562–4155.
Yukon Kuskokwim Delta Alaska Native AIDS Project, Yukon Kuskokwim Health Corporation, PO Box 528, Bethel AK 99559. Tel: (907) 543–6190.

*Arizona*

Fort Defiance Area Native American AIDS Education Project, Navajo Nation Family Planning Corporation, PO Box 1869, Window Rock AZ 86515. Tel: (602) 871–5092/5093.
Inter-Tribal Council of Arizona HIV/STD Program, 2214 N. Central, Suite 100, Phoenix AZ 85004. Tel: (602) 258–4822.
Native American Community Health Centers, Inc., Native American Pathways, 3008 N. 3rd Street, Phoenix AZ 85012. Tel: (602) 266–6363.
Native American HIV/AIDS Prevention Education Program, Northern Arizona Area Health Education Center, Inc., 2501 North 4th Street, Suite 9, Flagstaff AZ 86004. Tel: (602) 774–6687.
Navajo AIDS Network, PO Box 1313, Chinle AZ 86503. Tel: (520) 674–5676.

*California*

National Native American AIDS Prevention Center, 436 14th Street, Suite 1020, Oakland CA 94612. Tel: (510) 444–2051.
Native American AIDS Project, 1540 Market St., Suite 425, San Francisco CA 94102. Tel: (415) 522–2406.
San Diego American Indian Health AIDS Program, 3812 Ray Street, San Diego CA 92104. Tel: (619) 298–9090.

## Colorado

AIDS Education and Prevention Project, American Indian Health Care Association, 1999 Broadway, Suite 2530, Denver CO 80202. Tel: (303) 295-3788.

Eagle Lodge, Inc. American Indian Behavioral Health Treatment Services, 2801 East Colfax Avenue, Suite 306, Denver CO 80206-1540. Tel: (303) 329-6789.

Two-Spirit Society, PO Box 7523, Boulder CO 80306-7523. Tel: (303) 444-9009; (800) 337-1505. Fax: (303) 938-0299.

## Hawaii

Ke Ola Mamo, 1130 N. Nimitz, Suite A-221, Honolulu HI 96817. Tel: (808) 533-0035.

Papa Ola Lokahi, 222 Merchant St., 2nd Floor, Honolulu HI 96813. Tel: (808) 536-9453.

## Iowa

Winnebago Healthy Start, PO Box 3704, Sioux City IA 51102. Tel: (712) 252-5902.

## Minnesota

Minnesota American Indian AIDS Task Force, 1433 E. Franklin Ave., Suite 19, Minneapolis MN 55404. Tel: (612) 870-1723.

Walking the Wellness Path: HIV/AIDS, Program of Indian Health Board of Minneapolis, 1315 E. 24th Street, Minneapolis MN 55404. Tel: (612) 721-9879.

## Missouri

Native American Health/AIDS Coalition, 6025 Prospect, Suite 103, Kansas City MO 64130. Tel: (816) 333-7500.

## Montana

Blackfeet Service Unit, PO Box 760, Browning MT 59417. Tel: (406) 338-6154.

Crow Agency Community Health, PO Box 194, Pryor MT 59066. Tel: (406) 638-3461.

Fort Belknap Tribal Health Department, RR 1, Box 66, Harlem MT 59526. Tel: (406) 353-2651.

Fort Peck Tribe, Ft. Peck Tribal Health, PO Box 1209, Poplar MT 59255. Tel: (406) 768-3491.

Montana State Health Office, STD/HIV Education, 1400 Broadway, Rm. 305, Helena MT 59620. Tel: (406) 444-5900.

Montana United Indian Association, 105 Smelter Ave. N.E., Helena MT 59404. Tel: (406) 771-8722.

Northern Cheyenne Board of Health, Health Education/Tribal Health, PO Box 67, Lame Deer MT 59043. Tel: (406) 477-6700.

Rocky Boy Health Board, Rocky Boy Route, Box Elder MT 59521. Tel: (406) 395-4064.

Salish Kootenai Tribe, Tribal Health and Human Services, PO Box 280, St. Ignatius MT 59865. Tel: (406) 745-2411.

## New Mexico

Albuquerque Area Indian Health Board, Inc., HIV/AIDS Prevention Program. 2309 Renard Place S.E., Suite 10, Albuquerque NM 87106. Tel: (505) 764-0036.

## New York

ACT NOW – Akwesasne HIV/AIDS Information and Resource Center, Box 747, Hogansburg NY 13655. Tel: (518) 358-2001.

AICH Outreach Education Coordinator Network, 306 South Salina Street, Suite 201, Syracuse NY 13202. Tel: (315) 478-3767.

American Indian Community House HIV/AIDS Project, 708 Broadway, 8th Floor, New York NY 10003. Tel: (212) 598-0100.

American Indian Community House, Inc., 404 Lafayette Street, 2nd Floor, New York NY 10003. Tel: (212) 598-0100.

Native American Community Services, 2495 Main Street, Suite 524, Buffalo NY 14214. Tel: (716) 832-2303.

Native American Community Services of Erie and Niagara Counties, 1005 Grant Street, Buffalo NY 14207. Tel: (716) 874-4460; and PO Box 2161, 561 Portage Road, Suite 329, Niagara Falls NY 14301 Tel: (716) 282-5441.

## North Carolina

Borderbelt AIDS Resources Team, PO Box 945, Lumberton NC 28359. Tel: (910) 739-6167.

## North Dakota

Spirit Lake Sioux Tribe, Health Education Program, Tribal Health Office. 398 Fort Totten ND 58335. Tel: (701) 766–4236.

Standing Rock Sioux Tribe, Health Education Program, PO Box D, Fort Yates ND 58538. Tel: (701) 854–7474.

## Oklahoma

Ahalaya Native Care Center, Inc., 1211 N. Shartel, Suite 404, Oklahoma City OK 73103. Tel: (405) 631–9988.

Ahalaya Native Care Center, Inc., 3507 E. Admiral Place, Tulsa OK 74115. Tel: (918) 834–8136.

## Oregon

Northwest Portland Area Indian Health Board: Project Red Talon, 520 S.W. Harrison St., Suite 335, Portland OR 97201. Tel: (503) 228–4185.

## Pennsylvania

Choctaw Health Risk Reduction Education Project, Mississippi Band of Choctaw Health Department, PO Box 6020, Choctaw Branch, Philadelphia PA 38350. Tel: (601) 656–2211.

## South Dakota

Dakota Tribal AIDS Education Prevention Project, Council of Seven Fires, Rte. 2, Box 173, Flandreau SD 57104. Tel: (605) 997–2105.

Native American Women's Health Education Resource Center, PO Box 572, Lake Andes, SD 57356. Tel: (605) 487–7072.

## Wisconsin

Rainbow Community, Milwaukee Indian Health Board, 930 N. 27th Street, Milwaukee WI 53208. Tel: (414) 937–6600.

Centers for Disease Control National AIDS Hotline. Tel: (800) 342-AIDS
Centers for Disease Control National STDS Hotline. Tel: 1 (800) 227–8922
National Minority AIDS Council. Tel: (202) 483–6622.

## ANNUAL CONFERENCES

Indian Health Service Research Conference. Tel: (505) 248–4142.
Indigenous Nations HIV/AIDS Conference. Tel: (510) 444–2051.
Minority Health Conference. Tel: (313) 763–8093.
National Indian Health Board Conference. Tel: (303) 759–3075.
National Minority AIDS Council Conference. Tel: (202) 483–6622.

## WEB SITES

Centers for Disease Control and Prevention. *www.cdc.gov.*
Indian Health Service. *www.ihs.gov.*
National Minority AIDS Council. *www.nmac.org.*
National Native American AIDS Prevention Center. *www.nnaapc.org.*
Office of Minority Health. *www.omhrc.gov.*

# NOTES

INTRODUCTION

1. Thornton, *American Indian Holocaust,* 133.

2. Thornton, *American Indian Holocaust,* 44–45.

3. Thornton, *American Indian Holocaust,* 45.

4. Thornton, *American Indian Holocaust,* 43–45.

5. Thornton, *American Indian Holocaust,* 62–64.

6. Thornton, *American Indian Holocaust,* 64.

7. Satcher, "Surgeon General Calls for Action."

8. Prucha, *Great Father,* 293.

9. Prucha, *Great Father,* 330.

10. Rowell, "Native Americans, Stereotypes, and HIV/AIDS," 12–13.

11. Asetoyer, interview.

12. Roberts, "AIDS Could Wipe Out Small Tribes."

13. Hill, "Indian Country Health Care"; Meckler, "Long-Neglected Indian Health Service."

14. Centers for Disease Control and Prevention, *Progress in Prevention,* 2.

15. U.S. Department of Health and Human Services, "Racial and Ethnic Health Disparities."

16. Centers for Disease Control and Prevention, *Surveillance Report,* year-end 1999, 5.

17. Centers for Disease Control and Prevention, *Progress in Prevention,* 8.

18. Walters and Simoni, "Trauma, Substance Use, and HIV Risk," 238.

19. U.S. Department of Health and Human Services, *Native Americans and HIV,* 17–29.

20. Tafoya, "Pulling Coyote's Tale," 283.

21. National Native American AIDS Prevention Center, "Contrary to the Press Coverage," 1.

22. Satcher, "Surgeon General Calls for Action."

23. Centers for Disease Control and Prevention, *Surveillance Report,* year-end 1999, 16.

24. Rowell, "American Indians and Civilization," 1–7.

25. "AIDS Rates among Indians," 1.

26. McCarthy, "Myth of the Drunken Indian," 10.

27. Rowell, "Alcohol and AIDS," 1.

28. Gregory, "Much Remains to Be Done," 89.

29. Jennings and Asetoyer, *Impact of AIDS*, 7.

30. American Association for World Health, *Be a Force for Change*, 31.

31. Farmer, Connors, and Simmons, *Women, Poverty and AIDS*.

32. U.S. Department of Health and Human Services, *Indian Health Service*, 24–25.

33. Farmer, *Infections and Inequalities*, 91.

34. Rowell, "Future of Indigenous Health," 124.

35. Centers for Disease Control and Prevention, "Diabetes at Highest Levels."

36. Centers for Disease Control and Prevention, "Prevalence of Diabetes," 1.

37. Indian Health Service, *1997 Trends in Indian Health*, 117.

38. Jennings and Asetoyer, *Impact of AIDS*, 17.

39. Jennings and Asetoyer, *Impact of AIDS*, 11; Indian Health Service, *1997 Trends in Indian Health*, 6.

40. National Commission on AIDS, "Challenge of HIV/AIDS," 7.

41. American Association for World Health, *Be a Force for Change*, 31.

42. Centers for Disease Control and Prevention, "Prevention and Treatment of Tuberculosis," 4, 6.

43. Rowell and Bouey, "Update on HIV/AIDS," 51–52.

44. Tafoya, "Pulling Coyote's Tale," 287.

45. Robin, Chester, and Goldman, "Cumulative Trauma," 239–53.

46. Bouey and Duran, "Ahalya Case-Management Program."

47. Talvi, "Silent Epidemic," 9.

48. National Commission on AIDS, "Challenge of HIV/AIDS," 45.

49. Metler, Conway, and Stehr-Green, "AIDS Surveillance" 1470.

50. American Association for World Health, *Be a Force for Change*, 8.

51. American Association for World Health, *Be a Force for Change*, 8–9.

52. American Association for World Health, *Be a Force for Change*.

53. American Indian Community House, *Native American Leadership Response*, 57

54. Rowell, conversation with author.

55. Benoit, conversation with author.

1. NATIVE AMERICAN MEN AND HIV/AIDS

1. Jacobs, Thomas, and Lange, *Two-Spirit People;* Williams, *Spirit and the Flesh;* Lang, *Men as Women;* Roscoe, *Changing Ones.*

2. Jacobs, Thomas, and Lange, *Two-Spirit People*, 1–2.

3. Jacobs, Thomas, and Lange, *Two-Spirit People*, 12.

4. Brown, *Two Spirit People*, xvii–xxiv.

5. Jacobs, Thomas, and Lange, *Two-Spirit People*, 107–8.

6. Williams, *Spirit and the Flesh*, 135–40.

7. Williams, *Spirit and the Flesh*, 163, 175–87; Roscoe, *Changing Ones*, 3–38.

8. Williams, *Spirit and the Flesh*, 9.

9. Williams, *Spirit and the Flesh.*

10. Roscoe, *Changing Ones*, 7, 17–19.

11. Roscoe, *Changing Ones*, 18; Rowell, HIV *Prevention*, 5; Tafoya and Wirth, "Native American Two-Spirit Men," 52.

12. Rowell, HIV *Prevention*, 12–19.

13. Lang, *Men as Women*, xiii–xviii.

14. Young, conversation with author.

15. Roscoe, *Changing Ones*, 109–12.

16. Williams, *Spirit and the Flesh*, 196–200.

17. Brown, *Two Spirit People*, 48.

18. Jacobs, Thomas, and Lange, *Two-Spirit People*, 212.

19. Brown, *Two Spirit People*, 89.

20. Roscoe, *Changing Ones*, 101.

21. U.S. Department of Health and Human Services, *Native Americans and* HIV, 149.

22. Rowell, "AIDS and Native Americans," 57.

23. Westberg, "AIDS in Indian Country," 64.

24. *Face to Face.*

25. Rowell, HIV *Prevention*, 5.

26. Asetoyer, interview.

27. Asetoyer, interview.

28. Brown, *Two Spirit People*, 90.

29. Thornton, Sandefur, and Grasmick, *Urbanization*, 14; Nagel, "American Indian Ethnic Renewal," 952.

30. Gregory, "Much Remains to be Done," 91.

31. Rowell, HIV *Prevention*, 7.

32. Jacobs, Thomas, and Lange, *Two-Spirit People*, 154.

33. Rush, HIV *Prevention*, 66.

34. Katz, "AIDS Epidemic in San Francisco," s41.

35. National Native American AIDS Prevention Center, "Contrary to the Press Coverage," 2.

36. San Francisco AIDS Foundation, "About AIDS."

37. Paradis, "Multicultural Identity and Gay Men," 302.

38. Sullivan, "Pathways to Infection," 243.

39. Brown, *Two Spirit People*, 89.

40. National Native American AIDS Prevention Center, "Contrary to the Press Coverage," 2.

41. Rowell, "AIDS and Native Americans," 58.

42. Walters, "Urban American Indian Identity," 1–2.

43. Jacobs, Thomas, and Lange, *Two-Spirit People*, 153; U.S. Department of Health and Human Services, *Native Americans and HIV*, 148; Rush, *HIV Prevention*, 66.

44. Roscoe, *Changing Ones*, 102–3.

45. "HIV/AIDS Project Director" 12–13.

46. American Indian Community House, *Native American Leadership Response*, 50.

47. Saunkeah, conversation with author.

48. Lewis, "Status Passages," 93.

49. *Face to Face*.

50. Robin, Chester, and Goldman, "Cumulative Trauma," 240.

51. Rush, *HIV Prevention*, 66.

52. Roscoe, *Changing Ones*, 108.

53. American Association for World Health, *Be a Force for Change*, 28.

54. Rowell and Kusterer, "Care of Substance Abusers," 96.

55. Rothblum and Bond, *Preventing Heterosexism*, 246.

56. Rowell and Kusterer, "Care of Substance Abusers," 91–94.

57. Rush, *HIV Prevention*, 66.

58. *Circle of Warriors*.

59. Urban Indian Health Board, "Native American Health."

60. Benoit, conversation with author.

61. Westberg, "Native Organizations Battle," 81.

62. American Indian Community House, *Native American Leadership Response*, 69.

63. Roscoe, *Changing Ones*, 105.

64. Casgraux, "AIDS in Indian Country."

65. American Indian Community House, *Native American Leadership Response*, 63, 77.

66. American Indian Community House, *Native American Leadership Response*, 63, 77.

67. Bouey and Duran, "Ahalaya Case-Management Program," 4.

68. Casgraux, "AIDS in Indian Country."

69. U.S. Department of Health and Human Services, *Native Americans and HIV*, 7.

70. Rush, *HIV Prevention*, 67.

71. *Circle of Warriors.*

72. Roscoe, *Changing Ones,* 106.

73. LaFavor, *American Indians against* HIV/AIDS.

74. Broken Leg, *American Indians against* HIV/AIDS.

75. Rush, HIV *Prevention,* 53.

76. Tafoya, "Pulling Coyote's Tale," 288.

77. Ramos, Shain, and Johnson, "Men I Mess With," 483.

78. Grossman, "At Risk, Infected, and Invisible," 14.

79. Grossman, "At Risk, Infected, and Invisible," 14–15.

80. Stall, "How to Lose," 686.

81. Miller, "Assisting Gay Men," 48–63.

82. Odets, "AIDS Education and Harm Reduction," 13.

83. Clatts, "All the King's Horses," 94; Odets, "AIDS Education and Harm Reduction," 13.

84. Odets, "AIDS Education and Harm Reduction," 13.

85. Young, interview.

86. Bouey, conversations with author.

87. Bouey and Duran, "Ahalaya Case-Management Program," 6.

88. National Native American AIDS Prevention Center, "Public Policy Priorities."

## 2. NATIVE AMERICAN WOMEN AND HIV/AIDS

1. Jaimes and Halsey, "American Indian Women," 311.

2. American Association for World Health, *Be a Force for Change,* 8; HIV InSite.

3. Farmer, Connors, and Simmons, *Women, Poverty and AIDS,* 4.

4. American Association for World Health, *Be a Force for Change,* 29; Centers for Disease Control and Prevention, *Surveillance Report,* year-end 1999, 20.

5. Stoller, *Lessons from the Damned,* 10.

6. Stoller, *Lessons from the Damned.*

7. Centers for Disease Control and Prevention, *Surveillance Report,* year-end 1999, 16.

8. "New and Notices."

9. Becenti, "WARNING!," 2.

10. Centers for Disease Control and Prevention, *Surveillance Report,* year-end 1999, 16.

11. Centers for Disease Control and Prevention, *Surveillance Report,* year-end 1999, 15.

12. Farmer, Connors, and Simmons, *Women, Poverty, and AIDS,* 47.

13. Farmer, Connors, and Simmons, *Women, Poverty, and AIDS*, 47; Sherr, Hankins, and Bennett, *AIDS as a Gender Issue*, 22.

14. Farmer, Connors, and Simmons, *Women, Poverty, and AIDS*, 47.

15. Whitmire, et al., *Childhood Trauma*, 4; Centers for Disease Control and Prevention, *Surveillance Report*, year-end 1998, 14.

16. Wyatt and Chin, "HIV and Ethnic Minority Women," 180.

17. Wyatt and Chin, "HIV and Ethnic Minority Women," 159–60.

18. Goldstein and Manlowe, *Gender Politics*, 157–58.

19. Jennings and Asetoyer, *Impact of AIDS*, 7.

20. American Association for World Health, *Be a Force for Change*, 31.

21. Long and Ankrah, *Women's Experiences with HIV/AIDS*, 190–91.

22. Jennings and Asetoyer, *Impact of AIDS*, 8.

23. Centers for Diseases Control, "HIV/AIDS among American Indians and Alaskan Natives," 158.

24. Indian Health Services, "STD Prevention and Control," 4.

25. Indian Health Services, "Controlling Sexually Transmitted Diseases," 1.

26. Rowell and Rush, "HIV and High-Risk Behaviors," 29–32.

27. Indian Health Services, "Controlling Sexually Transmitted Diseases," 1.

28. Jennings and Asetoyer, *Impact of AIDS*, 10.

29. Rowell and Rush, "HIV and High-Risk Behaviors," 29.

30. Indian Health Services, "Chlamydia Rates in the IHS," 6.

31. Farmer, Connors, and Simmons, *Women, Poverty, and AIDS*, 54.

32. Sherr et al., *AIDS as a Gender Issue*, 49.

33. Farmer, Connors, and Simmons, *Women, Poverty, and AIDS*, xx, xix.

34. U.S. Department of Health and Human Services, *Indian Health Service*, 25.

35. Farmer, Connors, and Simmons, *Women, Poverty, and AIDS*, 23.

36. Farmer, Connors, and Simmons, *Women, Poverty, and AIDS*, 23.

37. Farmer, Connors, and Simmons, *Women, Poverty, and AIDS*, 23.

38. Gohdes, Schraer, and Rith-Najarian, "Diabetes Prevention," S95.

39. Peterka, "Diabetics Learn to Live Healthy," A7.

40. Centers for Disease Control and Prevention, "Prevalence of Diabetes," 1.

41. Farmer, Connors, and Simmons, *Women, Poverty, and AIDS*, 254–61.

42. "AIDS Study Shows Drop," B8.

43. Edwards, "AIDS Deaths among Native Americans."

44. Farmer, Connors, and Simmons, *Women, Poverty, and AIDS*, 254–61.

45. San Francisco AIDS Foundation, "AIDS 101."

46. U.S. Census Bureau, "Census Fact for Native American Month."

47. Landsberg, "Patients Forgo Medical Care."

48. Farmer, Connors, and Simmons, *Women, Poverty, and AIDS*, 254.

49. Tompkins et al., "Motherhood in the Context of HIV Infection," 197–208.

50. Campbell, *Women, Families, and HIV/AIDS*, 146.

51. Farmer, Connors, and Simmons, *Women, Poverty, and AIDS*, 279.

52. *Circle of Warriors.*

53. Thomas, "Interview with Cordelia Thomas."

54. Goldstein and Manlowe, *Gender Politics*, 347.

55. U.S. Department of Health and Human Services, *Native Americans and HIV*, 155.

56. Asetoyer, interview.

57. Goldstein and Manlowe, *Gender Politics*, 190.

58. Roth and Hogan, "Negotiating Safer Practices," 127.

59. Farmer, *Infections and Inequalities*, 81–82.

60. Rand, *National Crime Victimization Survey Report.*

61. Cohen et al., "Domestic Violence and Childhood Sexual Abuse," 561.

62. Peterka, "Sacred Circle Responds to Abuse," B1.

63. Greenfeld and Smith, *American Indians and Crime*, 4.

64. Greenfeld and Smith, *American Indians and Crime.*

65. Peterka, "Sacred Circle Responds to Abuse," B2.

66. Asetoyer, interview.

67. Walters and Simoni, "Trauma, Substance Use, and HIV Risk," 236–48.

68. U.S. Department of Health and Human Services, *Native Americans and HIV*, 156.

69. Chester et al., "Grandmother Dishonored," 249–58.

70. Chester et al., "Grandmother Dishonored," 238; Campbell, *Women, Families, and HIV/AIDS*, 85.

71. Cohen et al., "Domestic Violence and Childhood Sexual Abuse," 560.

72. Cohen et al., "Domestic Violence and Childhood Sexual Abuse," 561.

73. Rothblum and Bond, *Preventing Heterosexism*, 219.

74. Goldstein and Manlowe, *Gender Politics*, 86–87.

75. Goldstein and Manlowe, *Gender Politics.*

76. Goldstein and Manlowe, *Gender Politics*, 90–91.

77. Stoller, *Lessons from the Damned*, 17–21.

78. Roth and Hogan, "Negotiating Safer Practices," 69–71.

79. Goldstein and Manlowe, *Gender Politics*, 97; Roth and Hogan, "Negotiating Safer Practices," 70.

80. Long and Ankrah, *Women's Experiences with HIV/AIDS*, 49–50.

81. Wilson, "How We Find Ourselves," 312.

82. Jennings and Asetoyer, *Impact of AIDS*, 12.

83. Goldstein and Manlowe, *Gender Politics*, 47.

84. Rowe, "Name-Affiliated HIV Testing," 6.

85. Thomas, "Interview with Cordelia Thomas," 6–7, 9.

86. Goldstein and Manlowe, *Gender Politics*, 210; Stevens, Tortu, and Coyle, *Women, Drug Use, and HIV Infections* 161–75.

87. Jennings and Asetoyer, *Impact of AIDS*, 17.

88. Claymore and Taylor, "Tribal Nations Face Disease," 27.

89. *Her Giveaway*.

90. LaFavor, *American Indians against HIV/AIDS*.

91. Goldstein and Manlowe, *Gender Politics*, 344.

92. Elm, conversation with author.

93. Asetoyer, interview.

94. Asetoyer, interview.

95. Asetoyer, interview.

96. *It Can Happen to Anybody; Mom and Sons Series*.


## 3. NATIVE AMERICAN YOUTH AND HIV/AIDS

1. Ryan and Futterman, *Lesbian and Gay Youth*, 103.

2. American Association for World Health, *Be a Force for Change*, 8.

3. American Association for World Health, *Be a Force for Change*, 8.7.

4. Advocates for Youth, *The Facts*.

5. Centers for Disease Control and Prevention, *Surveillance Report*, year-end 1999, 22–23.

6. U.S. Census Bureau, "Census Fact for Native American Month."

7. American Association for World Health, *Be a Force for Change*, 6.

8. American Association for World Health, *Be a Force for Change*, 7.

9. Centers for Disease Control and Prevention, *Surveillance Report*, midyear 1999, 21.

10. Centers for Disease Control and Prevention, *Surveillance Report*, year-end 1999, 5–6.

11. Rowell, "American Indians and Civilization," 5.

12. Rowell, "American Indians and Civilization," 6, 7.

13. Baldwin et al., "Developing Culturally Sensitive HIV-AIDS," 324.

14. American Association for World Health, *Be a Force for Change*, 25.

15. Sussman and Duffy, "Are We Forgetting," 384.

16. American Association for World Health, *Be a Force for Change*, 26.

17. Saewyc et al., "Demographics of Sexual Orientation," 591, 597.

18. Indian Health Services Web Page, "Key Facts," 2.

19. Ryan and Futterman, *Lesbian and Gay Youth*, 39.

20. Centers for Disease Control and Prevention, "Prevention and Treatment of Sexually Transmitted Diseases," 1.

21. National Commission on AIDS, "Preventing HIV/AIDS in Adolescents," 4.

22. Barney, "Profiles of American Indian Adolescent Concern," 316.

23. D'Andrea, "Concerns of Native American Youth," 177.

24. Edwards, "Among Native American Teenagers," 190–91.

25. Indian Health Service, "Native American Youth Health Survey," 4.

26. Asetoyer, interview.

27. Sussman and Duffy, "Are We Forgetting," 385.

28. Miller et al., "AIDS Knowledge and Attitudes," 250–51.

29. Claymore and Taylor, "Tribal Nations Face Disease," 29.

30. Advocates for Youth, *The Facts.*

31. Ryan and Futterman, *Lesbian and Gay Youth,* 106.

32. Campbell, *Women, Families, and HIV/AIDS,* 184–86.

33. Wexler, "AIDS Knowledge and Educational Preferences," 667–81.

34. National Commission on AIDS, "Preventing HIV/AIDS in Adolescents," 17.

35. National Commission on AIDS, "Preventing HIV/AIDS in Adolescents," 7.

36. Lichtenstein, "HIV Risk and Healthcare Attitudes," 118–20.

37. Centers for Disease Control and Prevention, "Youth Risk Behavior Surveillance," 26–28.

38. Beauvais et al., "Drug Use, Violence, and Victimization," 292–99.

39. Miller et al., "AIDS Knowledge and Attitudes," 251.

40. Saewyc et al., "Demographics of Sexual Orientation," 597.

41. Advocates for Youth, *HIV/STD Prevention and Young Men.*

42. "Darrell Joe," 4.

43. Advocates for Youth, *HIV/STD Prevention and Young Men.*

44. Advocates for Youth, *Adolescent Sexual Health.*

45. Advocates for Youth, *HIV/STD Prevention and Young Men.*

46. Mulrine, "Preventing Teen Suicide," 64.

47. Advocates for Youth, *HIV/STD Prevention and Young Men.*

48. Advocates for Youth, *Adolescent Sexual Health.*

49. Dinges and Duong-Tran, "Stressful Life Events," 487–502.

50. Lipschitz, "Suicide Prevention in Young Adults," 7.

51. Sullivan, "Pathways to Infection," 247.

52. "Darrell Joe," 5–6.

53. Lipschitz, "Suicide Prevention in Young Adults."

54. Armas, "Teen Drug Use Higher," B6.

55. National Commission on AIDS, "Preventing HIV/AIDS in Adolescents," 4.

56. American Association for World Health, *Be a Force for Change,* 25.

57. Beauvais and Trimble, "Alcohol and Drug Abuse Prevention."

58. Beauvais and Trimble, "Alcohol and Drug Abuse Prevention."

59. Lehto, "Life or Meth Walk," B2.

60. Asetoyer, interview.

61. Beauvais and LaBoueff, "Drug and Alcohol Abuse Intervention," 139–71.

62. Beauvais, "American Indian Youth and Alcohol," 61–65.

63. Beauvais, "American Indian Youth and Alcohol," 63–64.

64. O'Nell and Mitchell, "Alcohol Use among American Indian Adolescents," 565–78.

65. Madigan, conversation with author.

66. Ryan and Futterman, *Lesbian and Gay Youth*, 42–43.

67. Whitmire et al., *Childhood Trauma*, 10–12.

68. Manson et al., "Wounded Spirits, Ailing Hearts," 259.

69. Manson et al., "Wounded Spirits, Ailing Hearts," 264–72.

70. Blum et al, "American Indian – Alaska Native Youth Health," 1639–40.

71. Martis, conversation with author.

72. Indian Health Service, "Key Facts about Alaska Native Children," 1.

73. Advocates for Youth, *Young Women of Color*.

74. Advocates for Youth, *Young Women of Color*.

75. Campbell, *Women, Families, and HIV/AIDS*, 87–88.

76. "Darrell Joe," 5.

77. Katz, "AIDS Epidemic in San Francisco," s43.

78. "Darrell Joe."

79. Rowell, "Enhancement of Self-Esteem," 3–5.

80. Asetoyer, interview.

81. Berlin and Berman, "Theater, Peers and HIV Prevention," 9–14.

82. Wren et al., "Preventing the Spread of AIDS in Youth," 313.

83. American Indian Community House, *Native American Leadership Response*, 48.

84. American Indian Community House, "HIV/AIDS News," 19.

85. Thomas and Herne, "Generations Program Akwesasne Site," 19.

86. "Janice Wilson," *Seasons* (autumn 1995): 9.

87. Wren et al., "Preventing the Spread of AIDS in Youth," 314.

88. American Indian Community House, "HIV/AIDS News," 18, 20.

89. Indian Health Service, "Key Facts about Alaska Native Children," 1.

90. Indian Health Service, "Welcome to Alaska Area," 1.

91. Albers, "Tradition of Healing," 29.

92. Yukon-Kuskokwim Health Corporation, "Tribal Unity," 8.

93. Fisher, Cagle, and Wilson, "Drug Use and HIV Risk," 113–15.

94. Alaskan AIDS Assistance Association, *Reach Out*, 4.

95. Nenzel, "Healing Spirituality," 1.

96. "Website Gives Alaskans Access," 7.

97. National Commission on AIDS, "AIDS in Rural America."

98. N. Forbes, "State's Role in Suicide Prevention Programs," 235–49.

99. Albers, "Tradition of Healing," 99.

100. Alaska Native Health Board, "Welcome"

101. Alaska Native Health Board, "Welcome."

102. Alaska Native Health Board, "Welcome."

103. Kettl and Bixler, "Alcohol and Suicide in Alaska Natives," 34–45; Indian Health Service, "Key Facts About Alaska Native Children," 1.

104. Baker, "Suicide Among Ethnic Minority Elderly," 253–54.

105. N. Forbes, "State's Role in Suicide Prevention Programs," 235–49.

106. Yukon-Kuskokwim Health Corporation, "Tribal Unity," 10.

107. Farmer, *Infections and Inequalities*, 51.


4. NATIVE AMERICAN PREVENTION

1. Center for AIDS Prevention Studies, "HIV Prevention Programs Effective."

2. Thornton, Sandefur, and Grasmick, *Urbanization*, 101, 172.

3. Thornton, *American Indian Holocaust*, 101.

4. Center for AIDS Prevention Studies, "Minority Groups and Young Gay Men."

5. National Commission on AIDS, "Challenge of HIV/AIDS," 44.

6. Rowell, "American Indians and Civilization."

7. *In the Wind*, 4–6.

8. Rave, "Health Care Reform."

9. Rowell, "Have We Met the Needs," 4.

10. U.S. Department of Health and Human Services, *National Minority HIV Institute Recommendations;* U.S. Department of Health and Human Services, *National Minority HIV Institute Proceedings*.

11. National Minority HIV Working Group, *Report to the Secretary*, 25, 34–35.

12. Public Law 101–391.

13. National Native American AIDS Prevention Center, "Comments to the HRSA."

14. The Ryan White CARE Act Amendments of 1996.

15. Public Law 104–146.

16. National Native American AIDS Prevention Center, "Comments to the HRSA."

17. National Native American AIDS Prevention Center, "Comments to the HRSA."

18. Rowell, "AIDS and Native Americans," 32.

19. U.S. Department of Health and Human Services, *Native Americans and HIV*, 35.

20. DePoy and Bolduc "AIDS Prevention," 51–69; LeMaster and Connell, "Health Education Interventions," 532; Peterka, "AIDS, the Silent Killer," B4; Armstrong,

"HIV Victim Finds New Meaning to Life," A6; Bindell, "Cultural Values Best Preventative Measure"; Lentz, "Fighting AIDS with Tradition."

21. Rowell, *HIV Prevention;* Rush, *HIV Prevention;* Mangum, Rush, and Sanabria, *HIV Prevention;* LaFromboise, Trimble, and Mohatt, "Counseling Intervention."

22. Center for AIDS Prevention Studies, "Characteristics of HIV Education."

23. Center for AIDS Prevention Studies, "Characteristics of HIV Education."

# BIBLIOGRAPHY

Advocates for Youth. *The Facts: Adolescents, HIV/AIDS and other STDs.* Washington DC: Advocates for Youth, November 1998.

————. *Issues at a Glance: Adolescent Sexual Health and the Dynamics of Oppression: A Call for Cultural Competency.* Washington DC: Advocates for Youth, February 1999.

————. *Issues at a Glance: HIV/STD Prevention and Young Men Who Have Sex with Men.* Washington DC: Advocates for Youth, February 1999.

————. *Issues at a Glance: Young Women of Color and Their Risk for HIV/STD Infection.* Washington DC: Advocates for Youth, December 1998.

*AIDS and the Native American Family.* Produced by Upstream Productions. Directed by Sandra Osawa. 11 min. Los Angeles County AIDS Program Office, 1990. Video-cassette.

"AIDS Rates among Indians, Alaskan Natives Mirror White Rates." *http://www.nando.net.* 5 March 1998. Printed 17 March 2000.

"AIDS Study Shows Drop of 26 percent in Mortality Rate." *Wall Street Journal,* 12 September 1997, B8.

Alaskan AIDS Assistance Association, *Reach Out Across the Myths to People, Disease, Life Booklet,* fall 1998.

Alaska Native Health Board. "Welcome to the Alaska Native Health Board On-Line!" 1999. *http://www.anhb.org.* Printed 17 March 2000.

Albers, Dave. "A Tradition of Healing: Alaskan Natives Bring Modern Know-How and Cultural Values Together to Improve Health Care in Rural Villages across the State." *Alaska Airlines Magazine* (August 1999): 27–30, 99–104.

American Association for World Health. *Be a Force for Change: 1998 World AIDS Day Resource Booklet.* Washington DC: American Association for World Health, 1998.

American Indian Community House. *A Native American Leadership Response to HIV and AIDS.* A Community Development Initiative. New York: Funded by the New York Department of Health AIDS Institute, 1994.

American Indian Community House. "HIV/AIDS News." *The American Indian Community House Community Bulletin* 15 (winter 1999): 18–21.

Armas, Genaro C. "Teen Drug Use Higher in Rural Areas than Big Cities." *Coloradoan,* 27 January 2000, B6.

Armstrong, Deanna. "HIV Victim Finds New Meaning to Life: Ministry Strengthens Goals, Spirituality." *Indian Country Today,* 30 November–7 December 1998, A6.

Asetoyer, Charon. Interview by Monica Clark. Yankton Sioux Reservation SD, 6 August 1999.

Baker, F. M. "Suicide Among Ethnic Minority Elderly: A Statistical and Psychosocial Perspective." *Journal of Geriatric Psychiatry* 27 (1994): 241–64.

Baldwin, Julie A., Jon E. Rolf, Jeannette Johnson, Jeremy Bowers, Christine Benally, and Robert T. Trotter II. "Developing Culturally Sensitive HIV-AIDS and Substance Abuse Prevention Curricula for Native American Youth." *Journal of School Health* 9 (November 1996): 322–28.

Barney, David D. "Profiles of American Indian Adolescent Concern about AIDS." *Tenth International Conference on AIDS: International Conference on STD.* Yokohama, Japan, 7–12 August 1994.

Beauvais, Fred. "American Indian Youth and Alcohol: A Study in Perplexity and Ambivalence." *Journal of the Alcoholic Beverage Medical Research Foundation* 8 (fall 1998): 61–65.

Beauvais, Fred, Ernest L. Chavez, Eugene R. Oetting, Jerry L. Deffenbacher, and Greg R. Cornell. "Drug Use, Violence, and Victimization among White Americans, Mexican American, and American Indian Dropouts, Students with Academic Problems, and Students in Good Academic Standing." *Journal of Counseling Psychology* 43 (1996): 292–99.

Beauvais, Fred, and Steve La Boueff. "Drug and Alcohol Abuse Intervention in American Indian Communities." *The International Journal of the Addictions* 20 (1985): 139–71.

Beauvais, Fred, and Joseph Trimble. "The Effectiveness of Alcohol and Drug Abuse Prevention among American Indian Youth." In press.

Becenti, Deenise. "WARNING! 3 Pregnant Native American Women Test HIV Positive." *In the Wind* 10 (spring 1999): 2.

Bedard, Paul. "ADD AIDS to Clinton's Legacy." *U.S. News and World Report* 128 (3 January/10 January 2000): 8.

Benoit, Joan. Director of the Native American AIDS Project. Conversation with author. San Francisco CA. 12 April 2000.

Berlin, Cydelle, and Laura A. Berman. "Theater, Peers and HIV Prevention: A Model." *FLEducator* (fall 1995): 9–14.

Bindell, Stan. "Cultural Values Best Preventative Measure for AIDS." *Indian Country Today,* 30 April 1995, PG.

Blum, Robert W., Brian Harmon, Linda Harris, Lois Bergeisen and Michael D. Resnick. "American Indian – Alaska Native Youth Health." *Journal of American Medical Association* 267 (25 March 1992): 1637–44.

Bouey, Paul. Director of Research and Evaluation, NNAAPC. Conversations with author. Summer 1997 and October 1997.

Bouey, Paul, and Betty E. S. Duran. "The Ahalya Case-Management Program for HIV-infected American Indians, Alaska Natives, and Native Hawaiians: Quantitative and Qualitative Evaluation of Impacts." Unpublished paper, National Native American AIDS Prevention Center, 1998.

Broken Leg, Martin. *American Indians against HIV/AIDS Leadership Project: Presentation by Martin Broken Leg.* University of North Dakota Department of Family Medicine. 126 min. Grand Forks MN, 1991. Videocassette.

Brown, Lester B., ed. *Two Spirit People: American Indian Lesbian Women and Gay Men.* New York: Haworth, 1997.

Cambridge, Charles. "Anthropologist Warns of AIDS Epidemic among American Indian People." Ph.D. Diss., University of Colorado, Boulder, 1994.

Campbell, Carole. *Women, Families, and HIV/AIDS: A Sociological Perspective on the Epidemic in America.* Cambridge: Cambridge University Press, 1999.

Casgraux, Doug. "AIDS in Indian Country: Fear, Stereotypes, Bigotry, the Problems!" *Indian Country Today,* 24–31 May 1999, B1.

Center for AIDS Prevention Studies. CAPS News. "Minority Groups and Young Gay Men Have High and Worsening Rates of HIV: Prevention Research is Lacking, Say UCSF Researchers in New Report." *http://www.epibiostat.ucsf.edu/capsweb/otanews.html.* Printed 5 October 1994.

———. CAPS News. "UCSF Team Finds HIV Prevention Programs Can Be Effective – Results Challenge Popular Opinion on Failure Rate." *http://chanane.ucsf.edu/capsweb/choinews.* Printed 4 October 1994.

———. CAPS Prevention Toolbox. "What Are the Characteristics of HIV Education and Prevention Programs that Work and Do Not Work." *http://www.caps.ucsf.edu/capsweb/.* Printed summer 1997.

Centers for Disease Control and Prevention. "Diabetes at Highest Levels Ever in the U.S.: Minority Populations Especially Affected." CDC press release, 30 October 1997.

———. "HIV/AIDS among American Indians and Alaskan Natives – United States, 1981–1997." *Morbidity and Mortality Weekly Report* 47, 6 March 1998.

———. "HIV/AIDS among U.S. Women: Minority and Young Women at Continuing Risk." August 1999. *http://www.cdc.gov.*

———. "HIV/AIDS and U.S. Women Who Have Sex with Women (WSW)." August 1999. *http://www.cdc.gov.*

―――. "The HIV/AIDS Epidemic in the United States, 1997–1998." 28 December 1998. *http://www.cdc.gov.*

―――. *HIV/AIDS Surveillance Report, year-end edition* 10 (December 1998).

―――. *HIV/AIDS Surveillance Report, midyear edition* 11 (June 1999).

―――. *HIV/AIDS Surveillance Report, year-end edition* 11 (December 1999).

―――. "Prevalence of Diagnosed Diabetes among American Indians/Alaska Natives – United States, 1996." *Morbidity and Mortality Weekly Report* 47, 30 October 1998.

―――. "Prevention and Treatment of Sexually Transmitted Diseases as an HIV Prevention Strategy." CDC UPDATE, June 1998.

―――. "Prevention and Treatment of Tuberculosis among Patients Infected with Human Immunodeficiency Virus: Principles of Therapy and Revised Recommendation." *Morbidity and Mortality Weekly Report* 47, 30 October 1998.

―――. *Progress in Prevention: Research and Support for Community Action: HIV and Trends.* Washington DC: Government Printing Office, 1997.

―――. "Youth Risk Behavior Surveillance – National Alternative High School Youth Risk Behavior Survey, United States, 1998." *Morbidity and Mortality Weekly Report* 48 (28 October 1999).

Chester, Barbara, Robert W. Robin, Mary P. Koss, Joyce Lopez, and David Goldman. "Grandmother Dishonored: Violence against Women by Male Partners in American Indian Communities." *Violence and Victims* 9 (fall 1994): 249–58.

*Circle of Warriors.* Produced by Phil Lucas Productions. Directed by Phil Lucas. 27 min. National Native American AIDS Prevention Center, 1989. Videocassette.

Clatts, Michael C. "All the King's Horses and All the King's Men: Some Personal Reflections on Ten Years of AIDS Ethnography." *Human Organization* 53 (spring 1994): 93–95.

Claymore, Betty, and Marian A. Taylor. "AIDS – Tribal Nations Face the Newest Communicable Disease: An Aberdeen Area Perspective." *American Indian Culture and Research Journal* 13 (1989): 21–31.

Cohen, Mardge, Catherine Deamont, Susan Barkan, Jean Richardson, Mary Young, Susan Holman, Kathryn Anastos, Judth Cohen, and Sandra Melnick. "Domestic Violence and Childhood Sexual Abuse in HIV-infected Women and Women at Risk for HIV." *American Journal of Public Health* 90 (April 2000): 560–65.

Conway, George, Thomas Ambrose, Emmett Chase, E. Y. Hooper, Steven D. Helgerson, Patrick Johannes, Myrna R. Epstein, Brent A. McRae, Van P. Munn, Laverne Keevama, Stephen A. Raymond, Charles A Schable, Glen A. Satten, Lyle R. Petersen, and Timothy J. Dondero. "HIV Infection in American Indians and Alaska Natives: Surveys in the Indian Health Service." *Journal of Acquired Immune Deficiency Syndrome* 5 (1992): 803–9.

Crocker, Allen, Herbert J. Cohen, and Theodore A. Kastner. *HIV Infection and De-*

*velopmental Disabilities: A Resource for Service Providers.* Baltimore: Paul H. Brookes, 1992.

D'Andrea, Michael. "The Concerns of Native American Youth." *Journal of Multicultural Counseling and Development* 22 (July 1994): 173–81.

"Darrell Joe," *Seasons* (autumn 1995): 4–8.

David [pseud.]. Interview by author. Tape recording. San Francisco CA. 12 April 2000.

Debi [pseud.]. Interview by author. Tape recording. San Francisco CA, 11 April 2000.

DePoy, Elizabeth, and Claire Bolduc. "AIDS Prevention in a Rural Native American Population: An Empirical Approach to Program Development." *Journal of Multicultural Social Work* 2 (1992): 51–69.

Dinges, Norman G., and Quang Duong-Tran. "Stressful Life Events and Co-Occurring Depression, Substance Abuse and Suicidality among American Indian and Alaska Native Adolescents." *Culture, Medicine, and Psychiatry* 16 (1992/1993): 487–502.

Edwards, S. "Among Native American Teenagers, Sex Without Contraceptives is Common." *Family Planning Perspectives* 24 (July–August 1992): 189–91.

Edwards, Thomas. "AIDS Cases Are up all around Indian Country." *In the Wind* 8 (May/April 1997): 4.

———. "AIDS Deaths among Native Americans Drop by 32 Percent: Case Management Is One of Chief Causes." NNAAPC Online. *http://www.nnaapc.org/media/itw8ola/html.* Printed 9 October 1997.

Elm, Crissy. Director of American Indian Community House HIV/AIDS OEC Network Project. Conversation with author. New York NY. 28 February 2000.

Epple, Carolyn. "Coming to Terms with Navajo Nadleehi: A Critique of Berdach, 'Gay,' 'Alternate Gender,' and 'Two-Spirit.'" *American Ethnologist* 25 (1998): 267–90.

*Face to Face: Native Americans Living with the AIDS Virus.* Produced by Phil Lucas Productions. Directed by Phil Lucas. 45 min. Rural Alaska Community Action Program and Alaska Native Health Board, 1989. Videocassette.

Farmer, Paul. *Infections and Inequalities: The Modern Plagues.* Berkeley: University of California Press, 1999.

———. *Women, Poverty and AIDS: Sex, Drugs and Structural Violence.* Edited by Margaret Connors and Janie Simmons. Monroe ME: Common Courage, 1996.

Fisher, Dennis G., Henry H. Cagle, and Patricia J. Wilson. "Drug Use and HIV Risk in Alaska Natives." *Drugs and Society* 7 (1993): 107–17.

Forbes, Jack. "The Urban Tradition among Native Americans." *American Indian Culture and Research Journal* 22 (1998): 15–41.

Forbes, Norma E. "The State's Role in Suicide Prevention Programs for Alaska Native Youth." *American Indian and Alaska Native Mental Health Research* 4 (1994): 235–49.

Gardner, William, Susan G. Millstein, Brian L. Wilcox, eds. "Adolescents in the AIDS Epidemic Series." *New Directions for Child Development* 50 (winter 1990).

Geballe, Shelley, Janice Gruendel, and Warren Andiman, eds. *Forgotten Children of the AIDS Epidemic.* New Haven: Yale University Press, 1995.

Gohdes, Dorothy, Cynthia Schraer, and Stephen Rith-Najarian. "Diabetes Prevention in American Indian and Alaska Native: Where Are We in 1994?" *Diabetes Research and Clinical Practice* 34 (supplement 1996): s95-s100.

Goldstein, Nancy, and Jennifer L. Manlowe, eds. *The Gender Politics of HIV/AIDS in Women: Perspectives on the Pandemic in the United States.* New York: New York, 1997.

Gregory, Delores. "Much Remains to Be Done." *American Indian and Alaska Native Mental Health Research: Journal of the National Center* 4 (1992): 89–94.

Greenfeld, Lawrence, and Steven Smith. *American Indians and Crime.* U.S. Department of Justice. Office of Justice Programs. Bureau of Justice Statistics. *http://www.ojp.usdoj.gov/bjs/pub/ascii/aic.txt.* Printed 26 May 1999.

Grossman, Arnold H. "At Risk, Infected, and Invisible: Older Gay Men and HIV/AIDS." *Journal of the Association of Nurses in AIDS Care* 6 (November-December 1995): 13–19.

Gubiseh-Ayala, Diana. "HIV/AIDS Case Management." *American Indian Community House Bulletin* 14 (fall 1999): 18.

*Her Giveaway: A Spiritual Journey with AIDS.* Produced by Skyman-Smith. Directed by Mona Smith. 22 min. Women Make Movies, 1987. Videocassette.

Higbee, Rebecca. CAPS News Web Site New Release. "Minority Groups and Young Gay Men Have High and Worsening Rates of HIV; Prevention Research Is Lacking, Says UCSF Researchers in New Report." *http://www/epibiostat.ucsf/capsweb/otanews.html.* Printed 18 August 1997.

Hill, Liz. "Indian Country Health Care Exhibits Broad Disparities: IHS Budgets Simply Don't Meet Needs." *Indian Country Today – Health* 29 March–15 April 1999, C1, C3.

"HIV/AIDS Project Director Wins Prestigious Award." NALCHA *News: Native American Leadership Commission on Health and AIDS* 6 (1998): 12–13.

HIV InSite. UCSF. "Key Topics – Women." *http://hivinsite.ucsf.edu/topics/women.* Printed 2 November 1998.

*I'm Not Afraid of Me.* Produced by Phil Lucas Productions. Directed by Phil Lucas. 29 min. Alaska Native Health Board, 1991. Videocassette

*In the Wind: HIV/AIDS in Native America* 9 (winter 97/98).

Indian Health Service. *1997 Trends in Indian Health.* Washington DC: Government Printing Office, 1997.

———. "Chlamydia Rates in the IHS." *The* IHS *Primary Care Provider* 23 (January 1998).

———. "Controlling Sexually Transmitted Diseases: An IHS Perspective." *The* IHS *Primary Care Provider* 23 (January 1998).

———. "Key Facts about Alaska Native Children and Youth." 26 January 2000, 1–2. *http//www/ihs.gov.*

———. "The State of Native American Youth Health Survey." February 1992, 1–39. *http//www/ihs.gov.*———. "STD Prevention and Control in the IHS: An Emphasis on Chlamydia." *The* IHS *Primary Care Provider* 23 (January 1998).

———. "Welcome to Alaska Area of the Indian Health Service." 20 January 2000, 1. *http//www/ihs.gov.*

*It Can Happen to Anybody.* Produced and directed by Charles Abourezk. 22 min. Native American Women's Health Education Resource Center, 1990. Videocassette.

Jacobs, Sue-Ellen, Wesley Thomas, and Sabine Lange, eds. *Two-Spirit People: Native American Gender Identity, Sexuality, and Spirituality.* Chicago: University of Illinois Press, 1997.

Jaimes, Annette M., and Theresa Halsey. "American Indian Women: At the Center of Indigenous Resistance in Contemporary North America." In *The State of Native America: Genocide, Colonization, and Resistance.* Boston: South End, 1992.

"Janice Wilson," *Seasons* (autumn 1995): 9–13.

Jennings, Jennifer, and Charon Asetoyer. *The Impact of* AIDS *in the Native American Community.* South Dakota: Native American Women's Health Education Resource Center, summer 1996.

Jordan [pseud.]. Interview by author. Tape recording. San Francisco CA. 11 April 2000.

Katz, Mitchell. "AIDS Epidemic in San Francisco Among Men who Report Sex with Men: Successes and Challenges of HIV Prevention." *Journal of Acquired Immune Deficiency Syndromes and Human Retrovirology* 14 (Supplement 2, 1997): s38–s46.

*Kecia: Words to Live by.* Produced and directed by Gryphon Productions. 30 min. Chariot Video Distribution, 1991. Videocassette.

Kettl, Paul, and Edward O. Bixler. "Alcohol and Suicide in Alaska Native." *American Indian and Alaska Native Mental Health Research* 5 (1993): 34–45.

Kubler-Ross, Elisabeth. AIDS: *The Ultimate Challenge.* New York: Collier, 1987, First Touchstone Edition, 1997.

LaFavor, Carole. *American Indians against* HIV/AIDS *Leadership Project: Presentation by Carole LaFavor.* University of North Dakota Department of Family Medicine. 40 min. Grand Forks MN, 1991. Videocassette.

LaFromboise, Teresa D., Joseph E. Trimble, and Gerald V. Mohatt. "Counseling Intervention and American Indian Tradition: An Integrative Approach." In *Ethnicity and Psychology: African, Asian, Latino, and Native-American Psychologies.* Edited by Kenneth P. Monteiro, 314–34. 1995. Revised, Dubuque IA: Kendall/ Hunt, 1996.

Land, Helen. "AIDS and Women of Color." *Families in Society: The Journal of Contemporary Human Services* 75 (June 1994): 355–61.

Landsberg, Mitchell. "Study Finds One-third of HIV Patients Forgo Medical Care." *Coloradoan,* 13 December 1999, sec. B.

Lang, Sabine. *Men as Women, Women as Men: Changing Gender in Native American Cultures.* Austin: University of Texas Press, 1998.

Lehto, Tesho. "Life or Meth Walk Elevates Addiction Concerns." *Indian Country Today,* 28 June–5 July 1999, B2.

LeMaster, Pamela L., and Cathleen M. Connell. "Health Education Interventions among Native Americans: A Review and Analysis." *Health Education Quarterly* 24 (winter 1994): 521–38.

Lentz, John. "Fighting AIDS with Tradition." *Indian Country Today,* 31 December 1995, PG.

Lewis, Jacqueline. "Status Passages: The Experience of HIV-Positive Gay Men." *Journal of Homosexuality* 37 (1999): 87–115.

Lichtenstein, Bronwen. "HIV Risk and Healthcare Attitudes among Detained Adolescents in Rural Alabama." *AIDS Patient Care and STDs* 14 (March 2000): 113–24.

Lieb, Loren E., George A. Conway, Micheal Hedderman, John Yao, and Peter R. Kerndt. "Racial Misclassification of American Indians with AIDS in Los Angeles County." *Journal of Acquired Immune Deficiency Syndromes* 5 (1992): 1137–41.

Lipschitz, Alan. "Suicide Prevention in Young Adults (Age 18–30)." *Suicide and Life-Threatening Behavior* 25 (spring 1995): 7.

*Lisa Tiger Story.* Produced by Harlan McKosato. Directed by Harlan. 27 min. 1993. Videocassette.

Long, D. Lynellyn, and E. Maxine Ankrah, eds. *Women's Experiences with HIV/AIDS: An International Perspective.* New York: Columbia University Press, 1996.

Madigan, Randy. Outreach Counselor for the Alaska Center for Alcohol and Drug Abuse Prevention. Conversation with author. Spring 1995.

Mangum, Anna, Andrea Green Rush, and Vince Sanabria. *HIV Prevention with Native American Youth: A Program Planning Manual.* Oakland CA: National Native American AIDS Prevention Center, 1994.

Manson, Spero, Janette Beals, Theresa O'Nell, Joan Piasecki, Donald Bechtold, Ellen Keane, and Monica Jones. "Wounded Spirits, Ailing Hearts: PTSD and Related Disorders Among American Indians." In *Ethnocultural Aspects of Posttraumatic*

*Stress Disorder: Issues, Research, and Clinical Applications.* Edited by Anthony J. Marsella et al., 255–93, 1996. Washington DC: American Psychology Association.

Martis, Kimberly, Esq. Conversation with author. Anchorage AK. 8 August 1999.

McCarthy, Michael. "The Myth of the Drunken Indian: Binge Drinking Reflects Behavior Learned on the Frontier, Not Inherited Traits." *Washington Post Health,* 22 September 1992, 10.

Meckler, Laura. "Long-Neglected Indian Health Service in for Budget Boost." *Los Angeles Times,* 15 January 1999.

Metler, Russ, George A. Conway, and Jeanette Stehr-Green. "AIDS Surveillance among American Indians and Alaska Natives." *American Journal of Pubic Health* 81 (November 1991): 1469–71.

Mike [pseud.]. Interview by author. Tape recording. San Francisco CA. 11 April 2000.

Miller, Robin L. "Assisting Gay Men to Maintain Safer Sex: An Evaluation of an AIDS Service Organization's Safer Sex Maintenance Program." *AIDS Education and Prevention* 2 (supplement 1995): 48–63.

Miller, William A., Paul Qualtere-Burcher, Caleb Lauber, Jeffrey P. Rockow, and Kay A. Bauman. "AIDS Knowledge and Attitudes among Adolescents in the Rural Southwest." *The Journal of Rural Health* 6 (July 1990): 246–55.

*Mom and Sons Series.* Produced by Circle Eagle Communications. 14:33 min. Native American Women's Health Education Resource Center. 1991. Videocassette.

Moore, Melinda K., and Martin L. Forst, eds. *AIDS Education: Reaching Diverse Populations.* Westport CT: Praeger, 1996.

Mulrine, Anna. "Preventing Teen Suicide: It Starts with Straight Talk." *U.S. News and World Report* 127 (20 December 1999): 64.

Nagel, Joane. "American Indian Ethnic Renewal: Politics and the Resurgence of Identity." *American Sociological Review* 60 (December 1995): 947–65.

National Commission on AIDS. HIV InSite, UCSF. "AIDS in Rural America." *http://hivinsite.ucsf.edu.* Printed 2 August 1999.

———. "The Challenge of HIV/AIDS in Communities of Color." Washington DC: Government Printing Office, December 1992.

———. HIV InSite, UCSF. "Preventing HIV/AIDS in Adolescents – June 1993." *http://hivinsite.ucsf.edu.* Printed 2 August 1999.

National Minority HIV Working Group. *Report to the Secretary on HIV/AIDS in Racial and Ethnic Communities.* Prepared by Velez Associates. Washington DC: Government Printing Office, February 1999.

National Native American AIDS Prevention Center. "Comments to the HRSA AIDS Advisory Committee Ryan White CARE Act Re-Authorization Workgroup." *http://www.nnaapc.org.* Printed 16 June 1999.

———. "Contrary to the Press Coverage of CDC's Report on AIDS in Native Americans, the Epidemic Is Not Leveling Off in Our Population." Oakland CA: National Native American AIDS Prevention Center, 1998.

———. "Native American AIDS Statistics – Year Ending December 1996." NNAAPC Fax Back, January 1997. Oakland CA: National Native American AIDS Prevention Center.

———. "Native American Women and HIV/AIDS." *Seasons* (winter 1997/1998).

———. "NNAAPC's 1999–2000 Public Policy Priorities." *http://www.nnaapc.org/priorities.htm.* Printed summer 1999.

Nenzel, Andrea Nenzel. "Healing Spirituality." *Four A's Newsline: the Newsletter of the Alaskan AIDS Assistance Association* (summer 1999): 1–2.

"New and Notices." *NALCHA News: Native American Leadership Commission on Health and AIDS* 6 (1998): 2–7.

Odets, Walt. "AIDS Education and Harm Reduction for Gay Men: Psychological Approaches for the Twenty-First Century." *AIDS and Public Policy Journal* 9 (1994): 3–13.

O'Nell, Theresa, and Christina M. Mitchell. "Alcohol Use Among American Indian Adolescents: the Role of Culture in Pathological Drinking." *Social Science and Medicine* 42 (1996): 565–78.

Paradis, Bruce A. "Multicultural Identity and Gay Men in the Era of AIDS." *American Journal of Orthopsychiatry* 67 (April 1997): 300–307.

Peterka, Jennifer. "AIDS, the Silent Killer, Can Be Prevented: the Eighth Leading Cause of Death in the United States Last Year." *Indian Country Today,* 31 December–28 January 1998, B4.

———. "Diabetics Learn to Live Healthy." *Indian Country Today,* 7–14 December 1998, A7.

———. "Sacred Circle Responds to Abuse: Batterers Learn that Women are Sacred." *Indian Country Today,* 14–21 December 1998, B1.

Prucha, Francis Paul. *The Great Father: The United States Government and the American Indians.* Lincoln: University of Nebraska Press, 1984.

Ramos, Reyes, Rochelle N. Shain, and Leonard Johnson. "'Men I Mess with Don't Have Anything to Do with AIDS': Using Ethno-Theory to Understand Sexual Risk Perception." *The Sociological Quarterly* 36 (1995): 483–504.

Rand, Michael. *A National Crime Victimization Survey Report.* U.S. Department of Justice. Office of Justice Programs. Bureau of Justice Statistics. *http://www.ojp.usdoj.gov/bjs/pub/ascii/cv97.txt.* Revised 1/13/99 from the 12/27/98 release. Printed 26 May 1999

Rave, Jodi. "Health Care Reform Inspires Consolidation: Nightmare for Native AIDS." *Indian Country Today,* 31 July 1994.

Reddy, Marlita A., ed. *Statistical Record of Native North Americans.* Detroit MI: Gale Research, 1993.

Regina [pseud.]. Interview by author. Tape recording. San Francisco CA. 4 April 2000.

Roberts, Chris. "AIDS Could Entirely Wipe Out Small Tribes, Researcher Says." *Boulder Daily,* 28 February 1992.

Robin, Robert W., Barbara Chester, and David Goldman. "Cumulative Trauma and PTSD in American Indian Communities." In *Ethnocultural Aspects of Posttraumatic Stress Disorder: Issues, Research, and Clinical Applications."* Edited by Anthony J. Marsella, Matthew J. Friedman, Ellen T. Gerrity, and Raymond M. Scurfield, 239–53. Washington DC: American Psychological Association, 1996.

Roscoe, Will. *Changing Ones: Third and Fourth Gender in Native North America.* New York: St. Martin's, 1998.

———. *The Zuni Man-Woman.* Albuquerque: University of New Mexico Press, 1991.

Roth, Nancy L., and Katie Hogan, eds. *Gendered Epidemic: Representations of Women in the Age of AIDS.* New York: Routledge, 1998.

Roth, Nancy L., and Linda K. Fuller, eds. *Women and AIDS: Negotiating Safer Practices, Care, and Representation.* Binghamton, NY: Harrington Park, 1998.

Rothblum, Esther D., and Lynne A. Bond, eds. *Preventing Heterosexism and Homophobia.* Thousand Oaks, CA: Sage, 1996.

Rowe, Gregory. "How Might Name-Affiliated HIV Testing Impact the Native Community." *In the Wind* 9 (fall 1998): 1, 6.

Rowell, Ron. "AIDS and Native Americans." *Winds of Change* 5 (spring 1990): 31–33.

———. "AIDS and Native Americans: New Battle with an Old Enemy." *Winds of Change* 5 (spring 1990): 56–58.

———. "Alcohol and AIDS." Native American HIV/AIDS Prevention Web Page. *http://www.sfo.com/~denglish/native-aids/seas_2.html.* Printed summer 1997.

———. "American Indians and Civilization: History and the Future of Native American Health." Keynote address at COMMON GROUND: Building Working Relationships with American Indian/Alaska Native Communities. Tempe AZ, 23–26 October 1999.

———. Conversation with author. Oakland, California. 10 April 2000.

———. "Enhancement of Self-Esteem: A Basis for High-Risk Behaviour Prevention." *AIDS Health Promotion Exchange* (1992): 3–5.

———. "The Future of Indigenous Health." *Current Issues in Public Health* 2 (1996): 124.

———. "Have We Met the Needs of the Communities We Attempt to Serve?" *AIDS LINK* 22 (March–May 1993): 1–4.

———. *HIV Prevention for Gay/Bisexual/Two-Spirit Native American Men: A Report of the National Leadership Development Workgroup for Gay/Bisexual/Two-Spirit*

*Native American Men.* Oakland CA: National Native American AIDS Prevention Center, 1996.

———. "Native Americans, Stereotypes, and HIV/AIDS: Our Continuing Struggle for Survival." *Siecus Report* 18 (February/March 1990): 9–15.

———. "Warning Signs: Intravenous Drug Abuse among American Indians/Alaskan Natives." *Drugs and Society* 5 (1990): 21–35.

Rowell, Ron, and Paul Bouey. "Update on HIV/AIDS among American Indians and Alaska Natives." *The IHS Primary Care Provider* 22 (April 1997).

Rowell, Ron, and Hannah Kusterer. "Care of HIV Infected Native American Substance Abusers." In *Counseling Chemically Dependent People with HIV Illness.* Edited by Michael Shernoff, 91–103. New York: Haworth, 1991.

Rush, Andrea Green. *HIV Prevention in Native American Communities: A Manual for Native American Health and Human Service Providers.* Oakland CA: National Native American AIDS Prevention Center, 1992.

Ryan, Caitlin, and Donna Futterman. *Lesbian and Gay Youth: Care and Counseling.* New York: Columbia University Press, 1998.

Saewyc, Elizabeth M., Carol L. Skoy, Linda H. Bearinger, Robert W. Blum, and Michael D. Resnick. "Demographics of Sexual Orientation among American-Indian Adolescents," *American Journal of Orthopsychiatry* 68 (October 1998): 5909–6000.

Sally [pseud.]. Interview by author. Tape recording. San Francisco CA. 4 April 2000.

San Francisco AIDS Foundation. "About AIDS: HIV/AIDS Statistics as of April 30, 1999." *http://www.sfaf.org/aboutaids/statistics/index.html.* Printed 5 June 1999.

———. "AIDS 101 – Women and HIV/AIDS." *http://www.sfaf.org/aboutaids/statistics/index.html.* Printed 4 November 1998.

Satcher, David. "Surgeon General Calls for Action on HIV/AIDS: In Crisis Proportions in American Indian and Alaska Native Communities." *Indian Country Today,* 17 May 2000, C1, C3.

Saunkeah, Bruce. National Native American AIDS Prevention Center. Conversation with author. Oakland CA. 10 April 2000.

Sherr, Lorraine, Catherine Hankins, and Lydia Bennett. *AIDS as a Gender Issue: Psychosocial Perspectives.* Exeter, U.K.: SRP, 1996.

Stall, Ron. "How to Lose the Fight Against AIDS among Gay Men." *British Medical Journal* 309 (July–December 1994): 685–86.

Stephen [pseud.]. Interview by author. Tape recording. San Francisco, CA. 11 April 2000.

Stevens, Sally J., Stephanie Tortu, and Susan L. Coyle, eds. *Women, Drug Use, and HIV Infections.* New York: Haworth, 1998.

Stoller, Nancy E. *Lessons from the Damned: Queers, Whores, and Junkies Respond to AIDS.* New York: Routledge, 1998.

Story, Mary, Karen F. Strauss, Elenora Zephier, and Brenda A. Broussard. "Nutritional concerns in American Indian and Alaska Native Children: Transition and Future Directions." *American Dietetic Association* 98 (February 1998): 170–76.

Sullivan, Carol. "Pathways to Infection: AIDS Vulnerability among the Navajo." *AIDS Education and Prevention* 3 (1991): 241–57.

Sussman, Todd, and Maureen Duffy. "Are We Forgetting About Gay Male Adolescents in AIDS-related Research and Prevention?" *Youth and Society* 27 (March 1996): 379–93.

Tafoya, Terry. "Pulling Coyote's Tale: Native American Sexuality and AIDS." In *Ethnicity and Psychology: African-, Asian-, Latino-, and Native-American Psychologies*. Edited by Kenneth P. Monteiro, 281–88, 1995. Revised, Dubuque IA: Kendall/Hunt, 1996.

Tafoya, Terry, and Douglas A. Wirth. "Native American Two-Spirit Men." *Journal of Gay and Lesbian Social Services* 5 (1996): 51–67.

Talvi, Silja J. A. "The Silent Epidemic: The Challenge of HIV Prevention within Communities of Color." *The Humanist* 57 (November/December 1997): 6–10.

Thomas, Cordelia. "Interview with Cordelia Thomas," *Seasons* (winter 1997/1998): 4–11.

Thomas, Sherril, and Lynn Herne. "Generations Program Akwesasne Site." *American Indian Community House Bulletin* 14 (fall 1999): 19.

Thornton, Russell. *American Indian Holocaust and Survival: A Population History Since 1492.* Norman: University of Oklahoma Press, 1987.

Thornton, Russell, Gary D. Sandefur, and Harold G. Grasmick. *The Urbanization of American Indians: A Critical Bibliography.* Bloomington: Indiana University Press, 1982.

Thurman, Pamela J., Barbara A. Plested, Ruth W. Edwards, Heather M. Helm, and Eugene R. Oetting. "Using the Community Readiness Model in Native Communities." CSAP Monograph. In press.

Tom [pseud.]. Interview by author. Tape recording. San Francisco CA. 12 April 2000.

Tompkins, Tanya L, Barbara Henker, Carol K. Whalen, Julie Axelrod, and Lisa K. Comer. "Motherhood in the Context of HIV infection: Reading Between the Numbers." *Cultural Diversity and Ethnic Minority Psychology* 5 (August 1999): 197–208.

Urban Indian Health Board, Inc. Native American Health Center Web Page. "Native American Health, Native American AIDS Project." *www.uihbi.org.* Printed 31 May 2000.

U.S. Census Web Site. Memorandum for Reporters, Editors, News Directors. "Census Fact for Native American Month, October 31, 1997." *http://www.census.gov.* Printed 20 July 1999.

U.S. Department of Health and Human Services. *Indian Health Service: Regional*

*Differences in Indian Health, 1996.* Washington DC: Government Printing Office, 1996.

————. Office of Minority Health. *National Minority HIV Institute Recommendations by Issue Area.* Prepared by Velez Associates. Washington DC: Government Printing Office, 11 October 1996.

————. *National Minority HIV Institute Proceedings Report.* Prepared by Velez Associates. Washington DC: Government Printing Office, 11 October 1996.

————. *Native Americans and HIV: Summary of Ongoing Special Projects of National Significance (SPNS).* Edited by Linda Burhansstipanov. Washington DC: Government Printing Office, Special Projects of National Significance, fall 1998.

————. "Racial and Ethnic Health Disparities." *http://raceandhealth.hhs.gov.* Printed 21 June 1999.

U.S. House. Report of the Select Committee on Children, Youth, and Families. *A Decade of Denial: Teens and AIDS in America.* 102 Cong., 2d sess. May 1992. H. Doc. 55–439.

Walters, Karina L., and Jane M. Simoni. "Trauma, Substance Use, and HIV Risk among Urban American Indian Women." *Cultural Diversity and Ethnic Minority Psychology* 5 (August 1999): 236–48.

————. "Urban American Indian Identity and Psychological Wellness." Ph.D. Diss. University of California, Los Angeles, 1995.

"Website Gives Alaskans across the State Access to HIV/AIDS Information." *Four A's Newsline: The Newsletter of the Alaskan AIDS Assistance Association* (summer 1999): 7.

Westberg, Jane. "AIDS in Indian Country, 'Being Part of the Circle:' An interview with David Young, an HIV-positive, Two-Spirited Man." *Winds of Change* 12 (autumn 1997): 82–84.

————. "Native Organizations Battle Against the Spread of AIDS." *Winds of Change* 12 (autumn 1997): 78–86.

————. "The Retreat." *Winds of Change* 12 (autumn 1997): 85.

Wexler, Sandra. "AIDS Knowledge and Educational Preferences of At-Risk Runaway/ Homeless and Incarcerated Youth." *Children and Youth Services Review* 19 (1997): 667–81.

Whitmire, Laura E., Lisa L. Harlow, Kathryn Quina and Patricia J. Morokoff. *Childhood Trauma and HIV Women at Risk.* Philadelphia: Brunner/Mazel, 1999.

Williams, Walter L. *The Spirit and the Flesh: Sexual Diversity in American Indian Culture.* Boston: Beacon, 1986, 1992.

Wilson, Alex. "How We Find Ourselves: Identity Development and Two-Spirit People." *Harvard Educational Review* 66 (summer 1996): 303–17.

Wren, Patricia A., Nancy K. Janz, Kathryn Carovano, Marc A. Zimmerman, and

Kathleen M. Washienko. "Preventing the Spread of AIDS in Youth: Principles of Practice from 11 Diverse Projects." *Journal of Adolescent Health* 21 (1977): 309–17.

Wyatt, Gail Elizabeth, and Dorothy Chin. "HIV and Ethnic Minority Women, Families, and Communities: An Overview." *Cultural Diversity and Ethnic Minority Psychology* 5 (August 1999): 179–82.

Young, David. Member of Two-Spirit Society. Conversation with author. Fort Collins CO. 30 May 2000.

Yukon-Kuskokwim Health Corporation. "Tribal Unity and Traditional Medicine Gathering VI, 6–8 April 1999." *The Messenger* 4 (6 May 1999): 1, 8–9.

# INDEX

Page numbers in *italics* indicate a figure.

*berdache,* 22
Bird, John, 55
bisexuality: lesbians and, 52; rate of, among Native Americans, 8, 68. *See also* gay/bisexual men
Blackfeet, 69
Broken Leg, Martin, 31
Bureau of Indian Affairs (BIA), 2
Byron, Barbara, 55, 79

California: Native population of, 25, 29–30; programs in, 73, 106; tribes unrecognized in, 29. *See also* National Native American AIDS Prevention Center; San Francisco, California
Cambridge, Charles, 2
Canada, 93
Cantil, Joe, 78
case studies: Darrell Joe, 68, 69, 73; David, 20–21; Debi, 37–39, 48, 49, 53, 54; Jordan, 15–17, 27; Kashka, 51; Mike, 60–62, 65, 67, 69, 71, 73; Nan, 49; Regina, 41–43, 48, 49, 50, 53, 54; Sally, 39–41, 48, 49, 53, 54; Stephen, 17–18, 25–26, 27; Tara, 52; Tom, 13–15, 26; Willie, 28
Centers for Disease Control and Prevention (CDC): contact information for, 109; ethnic minorities and spread of HIV/AIDS, 3; and lesbians, 52; misrepresentation of urban/rural AIDS cases by, 26; and youth, 64
Cheyenne, 21, 95
childcare, 56
childhood sexual abuse, 64, 71–72
children: breast-feeding and infection of, 63; care and support of, 56, 58; in case studies, 38, 39, 40, 41–43, 49; uninfected, born to infected women, 49. *See also* youth
Chippewa, 69
chlamydia trachomatis, 46–47
Choctaw, 35
Christianity: homophobia and, 22, 24, 36; interruption of traditions and, 22, 24, 33–34
cocaine, 68
co-factors. *See* risk factors
colonization: gender and sexual orientation variance and, 22, 36; HIV diagnosis as exacerbating effects of, 27
Colorado, 22, 33–34, 36, 89, 97, 106–7
coming out: and lesbian risk factors, 53; migration and, 25; and openness about diagnosis, 53
commercial sex. *See* prostitution
community: elders in, 31, 88, 97; family support in, 57–58; inability to discuss sexual

behavior by, 30, 31; involvement of, in education and outreach, 30–32, 73, 85, 87, 88, 90, 92; peer counseling and, 58. *See also* reservations; rural communities; traditions; tribes; urban communities
condoms: case studies referencing, 38, 50; language barriers and, 30; negotiation of use of, 50–51, 54, 71, 73–74; rate of use of, 50, 65; youth and, 65–66, 67–68, 71, 73–74
confidentiality: lack of, as risk factor, 8, 24, 53
contraception: use of, 65–66

database of HIV/AIDS clients, 34–35
death. *See* mortality rates; suicide
denial: as risk factor, 8
depression: gay/bisexual youth and, 69; and HIV diagnosis, 26–27; trauma and, 8; youth and, 69
diabetes, 6, 48, 70
diagnosis: adjustment to, 26–27, 40; case studies and, 14, 16, 17, 21, 38–39, 62, 69
diagnosis, failure to obtain: mistrust of government agencies and, 4, 8; and spread of AIDS, 26; for STDs, 47; stigma and, 4
diagnosis, sharing information about: case studies and, 16, 17, 39, 40, 42, 49; as coming out, 27; and fear of discrimination, 49, 58
diet: as risk factor, 6, 48
discrimination: fear of, and silence about diagnosis, 49, 58; HIV/AIDS services and, 28, 29; lesbians and, 52–53; poverty and, 49; in prison, 40; as risk factor, 28, 29, 52–53; two-spirits and, 23–25, 28, 29, 36; youth and, 68. *See also* education and outreach; homophobia; stigma of HIV/AIDS
diseases: diabetes, 6, 48, 70; rate of contraction of, 6; STDs (*see* sexually transmitted diseases); tuberculosis, 6–7. *See also* HIV/AIDS
diseases, introduced, 1–2; epidemics of, 1; history of lack of funding for, 81–82; mistrust of government agencies and, 8, 53; population drop and, 1–2; smallpox, 1–2, 8, 9, 81–82
domestic violence: case studies involving, 41–42, 50; condom use and, 50–51; and HIV/AIDS prevention program strategies, 92; posttraumatic stress disorder and, 51; rates of, 51; as risk factor, 8, 50–52. *See also* physical abuse; sexual abuse; violence
dropouts, high-school, 68
drug abuse: case studies involving, 14, 38, 39–43, 60; trauma and, 8; youth and, 68, 69–70, 71. *See also* intravenous drug use

drug/alcohol treatment: HIV education during, 27–28; rate of infection among patients in, 3

drug therapy for HIV/AIDS: in case studies, 15; and challenge of ongoing care, 29; cost of, and rate of infection, 9; false sense of complacency and, 18

*dubuds,* 21

Eagle Lodge Outpatient, 89

economics: migration and, 24, 25, 36. *See also* poverty

education and outreach: community involvement in, 30–32, 73, 85, 87, 88, 90, 92; elders and, 31, 88, 97; for gay/bisexual/two-spirit men, 18, 21–22, 30–36, 90–91, 92; homosexuality as cultural complexity in, 21–22; IHS and lack of, 2; and intravenous drug users, 92; lack of, as risk factor, 9; necessity of honesty in, 33, 64; NNAAPC and, 34–35; for older vs. younger gay men, 32; peer counseling as, 58, 73, 74–75, 83, 90; personnel shortages and, 77–78; reluctance to talk about sexuality as problem in, 30, 31; videos as, 55–56, 58–59, 79, 101–5; "white gay men" as focus of, 18; women and, 55–59, 92, 99; youth and, 66–67, 68, 70, 73–80, 88–89, 90, 93, 95, 97. *See also* discrimination; prevention

elders, 31, 88, 97

empowerment: Alaskan health services and, 78; condom use and, 50; rote guidelines vs., 33; by self, 33, 36; self-sufficiency and, 36; transgenders and, 90–91; women and, 57; youth and, 73, 74

Empowerment: A Strategy for HIV/AIDS Prevention and Access to Care Among Women of Color, 45

enrollment: lack of, as barrier, 4, 29, 40

epidemics: of introduced diseases, 1

Erie, 74

Eskimo, 76

ethnic minorities. *See* minorities

Europeans: diseases introduced by (*see* diseases, introduced); homophobia and, 22

family: rejection of children by, 64, 68–69; support of, 57–58. *See also* community

Farmer, Paul, 48, 54

federal policies. *See* government; Indian Health Service; tribes

Flathead Reservation, 96

focus groups, 96

Fort Peck Tribe, 89–90

Foundations of Indian Teens, 72

Four A's (Anchorage AK), 77

France, 22

Friendship House Association of American Indians, 27–28

funding: culturally appropriate programs and, 81, 83; examples of sources of, 86, 87, 88, 89, 90, 91, 92, 93, 94, 97, 98, 99; of IHS, 2, 3, 29, 58, 83; lack of, 30, 81–85; and NNAAPC, 34, 36, 86, 92; of Ryan White CARE Act, 35, 83–84

Gathering of Native Americans Model, 87

gay/bisexual men: bar scene as risk for, 27, 68; education and prevention and, 18, 21–22, 30–36, 90–91, 92; false sense of complacency in, 18; heterosexual behaviors among, 67; HIV/AIDS cases in, *19,* 19–20, *20;* love as factor for, 18; mortality rates of, 25; preconceived notions by and about, 32; as problematic term, 22; rate of infection in, 3, 82; rate of occurrence in Native Americans of, 8; youth, 19, 66, 68–70, 73. *See also* two-spirits

gender: AIDS cases by, *19;* and "biological sexism" of HIV/AIDS, 46, 49; defined, 21; differences in, and youth, 64; multiple/alternative, in Native societies, 21–23, 30; survival differences, 48–49. *See also* gay/bisexual men; two-spirits; women

gonorrhea, 46

government: funding by (*see* funding); migration as policy of, 24; mistrust of, 4, 8, 53; removal policies of, 24, 37, 41; termination policies of, 39, 40. *See also specific agencies*

Goze, Andrea, 75

Hall, Hakwireiosta (Leyosta), 74

Harris, Curtis, 26, 29

Harrison, Melvin, 23, 24, 26

Harry, Jodi, 26

Hawaii, 90, 95–96, 107

healing, traditional methods of, 28–29, 36, 62, 76, 77, 87, 98

health care: lack of adequate, as risk factor, 3, 9; lesbians and failure to seek, 52–53; personnel shortages in, 77–78; poverty and failure to seek, 49; women and failure to seek, 49, 52–53

health care, Indian: in Alaska, 8, 76–80; alternative methods used in, 55; decrease in

health care, Indian (*continued*)
funding for, 82–83; history of, 2–3; lack of adequate, as risk factor, 2, 3, 6, 8; lack of urban, 29–30; mistrust of government agencies and lack of, 8; traditional methods used in, 28–29, 36, 62, 77, 87, 98; transportation as issue in, 50, 78; youth and, 72. *See also* Indian Health Service
Health Resources and Services Administration (HRSA), 83
Health Survey of Indian Boarding Schools, 72
*hemaneh,* 21
hemophiliacs, *20,* 44
hepatitis, 13, 15, 70
*Her Giveaway* (video, Smith), 55, 56
heroin, 5
heterosexual transmission, 46, 53, 55, 63, 64, 92
high schools: alternative, 67–68; dropouts from, 68
Hispanics: number of HIV/AIDS cases among, 44–45, *45;* older sex partners of youth and, 72; rate of infection among, 3; and youth at risk, 64, 72
HIV/AIDS: as "biologically sexist," 46, 49; mislabeled as "white gay men's" disease, 18, 44; number of cases (*see* HIV/AIDS cases); potential to eradicate Native populations of, 1–2, 9; priority of, as low, 2–3; and survival rates, 48–49; tuberculosis combined with, 7. *See also* mortality rates; prevention; rate of infection; risk factors; stigma of HIV/AIDS
HIV/AIDS cases: in ethnic minorities, 44–45, *45;* funding tied to, as problematic, 82–85; in general population, *19;* in intravenous drug users, *20,* 20–21; in men, *19,* 19–20, *20, 45,* 45–46; in Native American population, *19,* 19–20, *20,* 25, 44–46, *45,* 82; in San Francisco, 25; in urban areas, 25, 26; in women, *19,* 44–46, *45;* in youth, *63,* 63, 65
HIV/AIDS services: discrimination and inaccessibility of, 28, 29; traditions of Native Americans utilized in, 28–29, 36, 62, 77, 87, 98. *See also* education and outreach; prevention; *specific groups and organizations*
homelessness: case studies involving, 14–15, 26, 38; youth and, 67
homophobia: imposition of Christian morals and, 22, 24, 36; as risk factor, 7–8, 23–24, 25, 68; youth and, 68. *See also* discrimination; stigma of HIV/AIDS
homosexuality: as cultural construction, 21–22. *See also* gay/bisexual men; lesbians; two-spirits
honesty, 33, 64
hospice care, 89
HRSA (Health Resources and Services Administration), 83
*hwame,* 21

identity: Indian, as complex, 4, 29; mixed-blood (*see* mixed-blood identity)
*I'm Not Afraid of Me* (video, Byron), 55, 79
Indian Health Service (IHS): in Alaska, 8, 76; confidentiality problems and, 8, 24, 53; and diabetes, 48; enrollment and access to, 4, 29; and establishment of programs addressing HIV/AIDS, 82; funding of, 2, 3, 29, 58, 83; lack of urban, 29–30; mistrust of, by Natives, 4, 8, 53; neglect of reporting by, 4; nonprioritization of HIV/AIDS by, 3, 23–24, 53; population served by, 8; problems in meeting needs of tribal people by, 2–3; and STDs, 47; and Sun Dance outreach, 58. *See also* health care, Indian
Indians. *See* Native Americans
inequality: as risk factor, 6, 43–44, 50, 54; and survival differences, 48–49
infection, deliberate. *See* diseases, introduced
infection rate. *See* rate of infection
Institute for Health Policy Studies, 85
intercourse. *See* heterosexual transmission; sexual behavior
*An Interruption in the Journey* (video, Smith), 55
Inter-Tribal Council of Arizona, 90
intimacy: need for, 16, 18, 25
intravenous drug use: in Alaska, 76–77; case studies referencing, 38, 39–40, 42; diabetics' needle sharing and, 6, 70; education and prevention strategies and, 92; and impacts on body, 5; Native people and myths about, 55; needle sharing and, 6, 20–21, 53; number of HIV/AIDS cases involving, *20,* 20–21; as risk factor, 5, 53–55; unprotected sex and, 5, 53, 54; women and, 5, 53–55, *54,* 76–77; youth and, 64
Inupiat, 47
Iowa, 98–99
isolation: as risk factor, 49–50, 68, 76, 77, 78, 85
*It Can Happen to Anybody* (video), 58–59

Jacob, Sue-Ellen, 21

Native American Women's Health Education Resource Center (South Dakota), 56–59; and STDS, 47; and transportation of patients, 50

Native Care HIV/AIDS Integrated Services Network, 35

The Native Women and Wellness Conference, 45

Navajos: circular migration and, 25–26; confidentiality and, 24; gender and sexual orientation among, 21, 23; homophobia among, 23; rate of infection among, 45; stigma of HIV/AIDS and, 75; suicide and, 69

*Navajo Times*, 45

Nebraska, 98–99

needle sharing, 6, 20–21, 53, 70

needs assessment survey, 94–95

Nevada, 90

New Mexico, 87

New York: awareness of destructive potential of HIV/AIDS in, 9; enrollment of Natives in, 29; programs in, 26, 56, 74, 75, 88–89, 93, 108; rate of infection in, 3; suicide rates in, 27, 69

Niagara, 74

NNAAPC. *See* National Native American AIDS Prevention Center

North Carolina, 108

North Dakota, 96–97, 108

Northern Cheyenne Board of Health, 95

Odets, Walt, 33

Ogitchidag Gikinoomaagad program, 75, 91

Oklahoma, 35–36, 53, 86–87

O'Nell, Theresa, 71

Oregon, 109

Osawa, Sandra, 56

outreach. *See* education and outreach

Pacific Islanders, 3, 44–45, *45*

Paiute, 21

Papa Ola Lokahi, 95–96

pap smears, 47

peer counseling/education, 58, 73, 74–75, 83, 90

Pennsylvania, 109

people of color. *See* minorities

personnel shortages, 77–78

physical abuse: two-spirits and, 28; youth and, 72. *See also* domestic violence; sexual abuse

Pike, Earl, 31

Pine Ridge Reservation, 23

policy: development of, 35

population: of California, 25, 29–30; of ethnic minorities, 3; and inaccuracies in racial reporting, 4, 94; introduced diseases and drop in, 1–2; served by IHS, 8; of uninfected children born to infected mothers, 49; urban vs. rural, 24. *See also* HIV/AIDS cases; mortality rates; rate of infection

*Positively Native*, 55

posttraumatic stress disorder, 27, 51, 72

poverty: difficulty of rising from, 37; discrimination and, 49; diseases and, 5–7, 47; migration and, 24, 25; as risk factor, 6, 9, 43, 47–50, 72; STDS and, 5–6, 47; survival rates and, 48–49; violent crime and, 50; women and, 43, 47–51, 54, 72; youth and, 72

powwows, 15, 18, 50–51, 90, 95

pregnancy, teen, 64, 65, 97. *See also* children; youth

prejudice. *See* discrimination

prevention programs: characteristics of effective, 83, 85–86; descriptive listing of culturally appropriate, 86–99; funding as issue in, 81–85; need for, 81; recommendations for culturally appropriate, 83, 85–86; research concerning minorities and, 82; research showing effectiveness of, 81; self-determination in, 83, 84, 85. *See also* education and outreach; safe sex

prison: case studies involving, 13–14, 26, 40, 41; discrimination within, 40; education and prevention in, 96; youth and, 67

prostitution: case studies involving, 14, 15, 38, 49, 61, 65; lesbians and, 52; two-spirits and, 27; violence and, 54; youth and, 61, 64, 65, 67, 71

psychiatric disorders, 26–27. *See also* depression

publications: services offering, 34

race: inaccuracies in reporting of, 4, 94

racism: two-spirits and, 28, 29. *See also* discrimination

rape: rate of, 51; youth and, 71

rate of infection: as declining in general population, 18, 19; in ethnic minorities, 3, 19, 82; in gay/bisexual men, 3, 82; in Native Americans, 3–4, 84; of STDS, 46–47, 65; of tuberculosis, 6–7; in women, 3, 4, 44, 64; worldwide, 9; in youth, 63–64. *See also* HIV/AIDS cases; mortality rates; risk factors

sterilization abuse, 53
stigma of HIV/AIDS: and failure to obtain
diagnosis, 4; and naming of informants in
text, 10; peer education and, 75; women and,
57. *See also* discrimination; homophobia
stigma of sexual orientation: youth and, 68–69
suicide, 26–27, 62, 69, 79
Sullivan, Carol, 69
Sun Dance, 58
survival rates, 48–49. *See also* mortality rates
sweats, 18, 62
sweetgrass, 29
syphilis, 46

Tafoya, Terry, 30, 31–32
*tainna wa'ippe*, 21
Talking Circles, 56
termination policies, 39, 40
testing: culturally appropriate prevention and,
86; lack of anonymous, as risk factor, 8, 30;
need for, 30
Tewa, 21
Texas, 41
theater, 74, 75
Thomas, Cordelia, 53
Tiger, Lisa, 55
touch: need for, 95
traditions: Christianity and interruption of,
22, 24, 33–34; denial of, in services offered,
29; disruption of, and suicide rate, 79; healing, in HIV/AIDS services offered, 28–29, 36,
62, 77, 87, 98; of multiple genders/sexual
orientation, 21–23, 97; passing on of healing, 76; prevention efforts in support of, 56,
85; Sun Dance, 58; Two-Spirit Society and,
33–34; women in, 43. *See also* community;
Native Americans; tribes
*Train the Trainers*, 92
transgenders: programs for, 90–91. *See also*
two-spirits
transmission: among lesbians, 52; heterosexual, 46, 53, 55, 63, 64, 92; through intravenous drug use (*see* intravenous drug use);
through unsafe sex (*see* unsafe sex)
transportation as issue, 50, 78
trauma: rates of, 51; as risk factor, 8, 51–52,
71–72; substance abuse and, 71. *See also*
domestic violence; sexual abuse
tribes: enrollment in, 4, 29, 40; funding
inadequacies and, 83–84; prevention strategies and heterogeneity of, 86; removal

policies involving, 24, 37, 41; termination
policies involving, 39, 40. *See also* community; Native Americans; traditions
Tri-Ethnic Center for Prevention Research
(Colorado), 31
tuberculosis, 6–7
*Two-Spirit People* (Jacob), 21
two-spirits: bar scene and, 27; Christianity
as affecting, 22, 24, 33–34, 36; discrimination against, 23–25, 28, 29, 36; educa-
tion/outreach/prevention and, 18, 21–22,
30–36, 90–91, 92; enrollment as barrier to
care for, 29; and gender and sexual orientation variances as tribal tradition, 21–23;
migration of, 24–26, 36; mortality rate and,
25; Native organizations serving, 34–36;
persecution of, 22; prostitution and, 27; risk
factors for, 27–28, 32; suicide and, 26–27;
as term, 9, 22; violence against, 23. *See also*
gay/bisexual men
Two-Spirit Society of Colorado, 22, 33–34, 36,
97
typhus, 1

*Uncle Jake's Story* (coloring book), 79
unemployment: migration and, 24; women
and, 47
United States Conference on AIDS, 74, 76, 82
University of California at San Francisco
(UCSF), 81, 85
unsafe sex: alcohol as risk factor for, 27; with
intravenous drug users, 5, 53, 54; youth
and, 65–66, 67, 69, 71. *See also* safe sexual
practices
urban communities: denial and, 8; funding
and, 83; high-risk behaviors and, 25–26;
HIV/AIDS cases in, 26; lack of IHS in, 29–30;
migration to (*see* migration); NNAAPC and,
36; prevention programs and, 92; women
and, 56; youth prevention materials and,
73. *See also* community; reservations; rural
communities
Urban Indian Health Center (San Francisco),
18, 28–29
U.S. National Commission on AIDS, 77
Utah, 90

vagina, vaginal secretions, 46
videos: prevention and, 55–56, 58–59, 79, 101–5
violence: drug-use lifestyle and, 54; against
lesbians, 52; prostitution and, 54; against